BURIED ALIVE

THE TRUE STORY OF KIDNAPPING, CAPTIVITY, AND A DRAMATIC RESCUE

ROY HALLUMS
WITH AUDREY HUDSON

THOMAS NELSON
Since 1798

NASHVILLE   DALLAS   MEXICO CITY   RIO DE JANEIRO

Published in Nashville, Tennessee, by Thomas Nelson. Thomas Nelson is a trademark of Thomas Nelson, Inc.

Thomas Nelson, Inc., titles may be purchased in bulk for educational, business, fund-raising, or sales promotional use. For information, please e-mail SpecialMarkets@ ThomasNelson.com.

ISBN 978-1-59555-548-9 (trade paper)

Library of Congress Cataloging-in-Publication Data

Hallums, Roy.
  Buried alive : the true story of kidnapping, captivity, and a dramatic rescue / Roy Hallums, with Audrey Hudson.
    p. cm.
  Includes bibliographical references and index.
  ISBN 978-1-59555-170-2 (hardcover) 1. Hallums, Roy. 2. Iraq War, 2003—Personal narratives, American. 3. Kidnapping victims—Iraq. I. Hudson, Audrey. II. Title.
  DS79.76.H34 2009
  946.7044'31—dc22
  [B]

2009021039

Printed in the United States of America

This book is dedicated to Carrie, Amanda,
Barbara, Sabrina, Susan, Steve, and Mike,
for their love and belief that I would truly
return home to them one day.

CONTENTS

INTRODUCTION

Victory is gained not by the number killed
but by the number frightened.

—ARAB PROVERB

B eginning around April 2004, being kidnapped and held hostage
was the single fear that terrorized Western journalists, international
aid workers, reconstruction contractors, diplomats, coalition soldiers, and local Iraqis alike in post-Saddam Iraq. Hostage-taking quickly
became the prevalent terrorist tactic to hinder the reconstruction effort,
damage diplomatic relations, fund the insurgency, and spread a message
of terror to the world.

Jihadist Web sites and Al Jazeera television aired video clips of Western
hostages, paraded in orange jumpsuits, Abu Ghraib–style, or on their
knees, begging for mercy, surrounded by *mujahideen* (Islamic warriors),
who pronounced judgment on the "infidels" before beheading them in
front of the cameras. These images put a new twist on the traditional terrorist maxim on assassinations: kidnap one, terrorize thousands.

Kidnapping was the link that connected all components of the security crisis and became integral to the post–Saddam Hussein story in Iraq
following the U.S.-led invasion. Multinational forces from more than
thirty countries made up the coalition of military peacekeeping and

reconstruction security forces in Iraq. This coalition bore the burden of responsibility for the postwar state of Iraq's fragile security situation.

However, the phenomenon of kidnapping long predates the arrival of foreign troops. For centuries it has been an illegal yet common practice in the Middle East to generate cash, embarrass enemies, or force political action.

Bedouin tribes used hostage-taking to acquire wives, to serve as bargaining chips in tribal negotiations, and to produce human chattel for slave trading. Both the Bible and the Koran reference the scheme, and kidnapping continues today as an abhorrent fact of life in many Middle Eastern societies.

With the ascendancy of Saddam Hussein's regime upon the Iraqi political landscape in 1979, the Ba'athists' security apparatus also adopted this malevolent practice as a terror tactic to be used against a helpless populace. During Saddam's twenty-four-year reign, hundreds of thousands of people disappeared under a widespread campaign of state-sponsored abductions and executions conducted to suppress political opposition. The full extent of Saddam's internal kidnapping campaign was never documented and will likely never be known, as all news was controlled through just one media outlet, run by his complicit son Uday.

Saddam issued an executive order on the eve of the coalition's invasion that released one hundred thousand convicts from Iraqi jails, flooding an already-deteriorating environment with potential perpetrators who already possessed the inherent skill sets of a hostage taker. These former prisoners were themselves victims of similar abuse and were thus prone to violence, with demonstrated criminal intent. Under these conditions, the explosion of hostage-taking incidents in Iraq was inevitable, as the practice was indigenous to preinvasion Iraqi society. The collapse of an authoritarian Arab police state and its subsequent occupation by a relatively limited number of Western forces resulted in a permissive environment primed for exploitation by insurgents, militias, and local criminals, creating a civil-war atmosphere.

Suicide bombings dominated the headlines daily, but kidnappings far outnumbered kinetic insurgent attacks against coalition forces and Iraqis alike. The continued absence of a credible central authority fostered a perpetual cycle of unchecked political violence, sectarian strife, insurgent attacks, and illegal activity of every stripe, in which everyone with a terrorist agenda or criminal intent used abduction to spread fear or to fund his retirement plan.

From the coalition's perspective, the situation was exacerbated by limited actionable intelligence collected on the perpetrators, as well as a populace committed to protecting tribal relations complicit in the crimes. The Iraqi public was paralyzed by the fear of reprisals, as most perpetrators used violence disproportionate to any perceived slight. A mostly ineffectual Iraqi military and corrupt police compounded these harsh realities; many times Iraqi security personnel were involved in the very kidnappings they were chartered to prevent. The threat did not abate, as hostage takers conducted their activities largely unaffected by coalition and Iraqi attempts to stem the problem.

In Iraq, where terrorism and criminality go hand in hand, the hostage takers sought monetary reward through intimidation and extortion. Many insurgent cells were comprised of former criminals and led by veterans of Saddam's army, including the ruthless Fedayeen Saddam and the much-feared Mukhabarat (Iraqi Intelligence Service). The relationship between terrorists and criminals regularly blurred. Hostage takers publicly claimed that they were motivated freedom fighters, calling for the release of prisoners or demanding that the victims' military or company pull out of Iraq. Yet privately, these kidnappers demanded high sums of money from families for the safe release of their loved ones. Therefore, kidnapping was a duplicitous trade in Iraq, with captors using the pretense of noble political activism to mask their real motivation: greed.

Kidnapping soon became the growth industry in Iraq for anyone with a car and a few friends with AK-47s. In a country where a good monthly salary was three hundred dollars net per month, the earning potential for kidnapping offered a viable low-risk and high-return alternative for individuals unwilling to take a chance with an irregular government paycheck. The typical snatch on the streets of Baghdad netted thousands of dollars, as desperate families were willing to sell everything they owned to save a kidnapped relative. For a foreigner, the asking price ranged from five hundred thousand to twelve million dollars. The ransom was usually determined by a victim's nationality or political status within the government or tribal pecking order. It was compounded by his country's reputation for conceding to this form of terrorism. In many cases, the company or country paid the lifesaving bill, because it was so far beyond the means of the average family. The willingness to pay only emboldened the hostage takers to target countries and firms who repeatedly paid these ransoms.

Those who wonder about the cost of a human life need only to look at the model Iraq provided. There was a market value on the Arab street that based the worth of a human life on one's nationality, gender, and profession. To save the life of an Iraqi's pride and joy, an elementary school–aged, firstborn son, the price averaged ten thousand dollars. Petty criminals and stateless terrorists could garner five *million* dollars for a female Western journalist by bringing acquiescent governments to their knees.

Kidnappings were largely viewed as a symptom, rather than a cause, of the security crisis in Iraq. But whether cause or symptom, widespread hostage-taking incidents systematically eroded every effort and undermined every goal the United States sought to achieve in the post-Saddam era. In fact, they became a metaphor for our failure to bring security, stability, and governance to Iraq. Kidnapping became one of the principal tools in the terrorist asymmetric arsenal of weapons of mass effect and was used with considerable success in Iraq. Generally viewed as isolated tactical events, overall their impact was catastrophic to the coalition strategy: since the onset of the insurgency, more than 450 foreigners have been taken hostage, and Iraqi victims number in the tens of thousands.

Rampant kidnappings also became a part of the postinvasion narrative of Iraq. The international media coverage of high-profile kidnapping cases created a propaganda windfall for those responsible, guaranteeing extremists a voice to communicate their agenda to a worldwide audience. Internet postings of kidnapping operations with hostages' pleas and subsequent murders, abhorred by the West, served as recruiting and fund-raising tools for their sympathizers in the Muslim world. The hostage takers intimidated the educated classes, effectively accelerating the displacement and emigration of Iraqi professionals—an effect analysts termed the "Iraqi brain drain."

Kidnappings also hijacked the reconstruction effort of the previously lauded but now much-maligned Marshall Plan for Iraq. Reconstruction benchmarks went unmet as contractors pulled out of the effort due to rising security costs and employee concerns. Masked kidnappers extracted strategic gains from coalition partners, including state-supported million-dollar ransoms, and the withdrawal of troops and diplomatic missions.

Who was the typical kidnapping victim in Iraq? Abductors targeted victims across ethnic, sectarian, and occupational sectors. Since 2003, kidnappers have taken foreign hostages from more than fifty countries that participated in the reconstruction effort. While Western victims were the focus of the major news outlets, Iraqis and other Arabs suffered this terror most often.

Second only to the number of local victims, neighbors from surrounding countries were targeted most frequently, accounting for more than 50 percent of all reported foreign kidnappings from April 2004 to 2006. Turkey, Jordan, Lebanon, and Egypt were all listed in the top five. Americans were number two among non-Iraqi victims. Although Westerners accounted for only a quarter of all incidents reported, these stories dominated the headlines.

In Iraq, kidnap victims were usually exchanged for tens of thousands and in some cases millions of dollars. Western hostages were typically sold up the chain for tens of thousands of dollars only to be ransomed later for millions to fund the insurgency. The unlucky ones were murdered at the hands of extremist terrorist networks usually linked to Al-Qaeda in Iraq.

It is no coincidence that the spike in kidnappings occurred during the period of Abu Musab al-Zarqawi's reign over the Al-Qaeda in Iraq network. Referred to as AMZ in military circles, Zarqawi used kidnappings to support his media campaign to engender terror throughout the world. He was identified as the knife-wielder in prominent beheading videos aired on Al Jazeera and other jihadist Internet media outlets. Overall, the insurgency successfully used the threat and killing of hostages to finance operations, recruit new followers, and garner strategic concessions.

One report revealed that in 2006, foreign governments including France, Germany, Italy, Romania, and the Philippines paid forty-five million dollars in ransoms. Other demands were met as concessions to terrorism: the Philippines pulled their troops out to save a hostage; Arab missions—including Pakistan, Bahrain, Sudan, and Egypt—recalled envoys from Baghdad after embassy staff members were kidnapped. These concessions and ransoms fueled and financed more kidnappings and insurgent attacks.

The official U.S. National Security Strategy policy is that the United States will make no concessions to terrorist demands and strike no deals with them. Paying ransoms is not an option for most Americans kidnapped in Iraq; rescue is their only hope. So, in response to the kidnapping crisis, the American Embassy in Baghdad established the Hostage Working Group (HWG) in the summer of 2004. The charter of the organization included taking "actions to deter, prevent, and be prepared to respond to hostage-taking incidents." The HWG's trifold priorities were to prevent kidnappings, rescue hostages, and bring those responsible to justice. Over time, due to direct and indirect efforts by the HWG, the military, police, and many others, the kidnapping crisis abated; kidnapping cells were rounded up and dismantled. But overall, the HWG would claim limited success on its loftiest goal—the safe recovery of hostage victims.

The postinvasion foreign kidnapping crisis in Iraq began April 9, 2004, when a thirty-vehicle supply convoy driving through the Abu Ghraib neighborhood west of Baghdad endured a five-mile-long ambush in which militants attacked and captured survivors. Among the hostages was a young American soldier from Batavia, Ohio, who later appeared in a proof-of-life video released on Al Jazeera on April 16. Identified as Private First Class Keith Matthew Maupin, he was reported missing in action and declared a prisoner of war. The military established Task Force Maupin, which investigated every lead; the assigned soldiers took a West African proverb, *Odo Nnyew Fie Kwan Frame* (Love never loses its way home), as the unit motto. Hundreds of intelligence reports were investigated while Maupin's parents, Keith and Carolyn, never gave up hope that Matt would come home. Nearly four years to the day of his original capture, Maupin's remains were recovered in Iraq; he was buried with full military honors on April 27, 2008. His memorial service was attended by his family, friends, and military peers.

Some hostages were luckier. In early January 2006, Jill Carroll, an American journalist writing for the *Christian Science Monitor*, was kidnapped immediately following an interview with an Iraqi politician in Baghdad. After a concentrated effort across military, intelligence, law enforcement, and public relations channels, her captors released Carroll after more than eighty-three days.

Between bookends of the two most-reported stories on Americans kidnapped in Iraq is the story of Roy Hallums—a tale for the spiritual soul, of how we found him and brought him home.

—Dan O'Shea

A Navy SEAL and commander in the U.S. Naval Reserves, O'Shea established and served as the Hostage Working Group coordinator at the U.S. Embassy–Baghdad from July 2004 to April 2006.

1

KIDNAPPED!

The traitor's name was Majid. He was one of several men armed with AK-47s whose job it was to protect my coworkers and me at the Saudi Arabian Trading and Construction Company in the upscale Mansour district of Baghdad during the height of the war in Iraq.

The other guards were grateful that warm November evening when Majid offered to stand watch alone at the gateway to our compound, an office building and a private home directly behind it that was surrounded on all sides by a concrete wall. It was the holy month of Ramadan, when Muslims fast from dawn to dusk, and as the sun was setting, it meant that the guards could escape the dust-filled air and head into the office's kitchen to prepare their first meal of the day. I was attending a dinner party given by the company owner, Malek Antabi, who was hosting the affair at the private home next to the office building.

In hindsight, I really wish I had learned to speak Arabic. I spent a great deal of time in the Middle East after I retired as a Naval commander with twenty years of service; I learned a lot about Arab culture and the religion of Islam, but I just didn't have an ear for the language. At the dinner party, all of the guests were speaking in their native language as we ate dates and drank small cups of Arabic coffee. I didn't know what in the world the men were talking about.

As dinner was a long way off, I told my colleague Zein Hussami that I was going to the office to work on some contracts. I asked him to come over and get me when the food was ready, and I headed to work. The rooftop route was the quickest way to go back and forth between the buildings—upstairs to the house's second floor, down a hallway, and through a door that led to a large rooftop patio used for social occasions. A metal bridge connected the house and office building, with about one foot of space separating the buildings; four steps up the bridge, across a short plank, and four steps down, and I was on the other rooftop patio. Crossing it, I opened the door that led to the second floor, where my office was located.

It may sound like a strange path to take, but in addition to being a shortcut, it was much safer than traveling the streets outside of the guarded compound walls. By taking the rooftop route, I avoided the courtyard in front of the office, where vehicles would enter the compound after being cleared by security through a metal gate. The gate that Majid was suppos-edly guarding.

As I crossed the rooftop, I didn't see anyone. I didn't hear anything, other than my stomach, which was rumbling as I settled into the chair in front of my desk to catch up on some e-mail and go over food con-tracts we were negotiating with the American Army. I kept an eye on my office doorway, hoping Zein would appear soon and announce that din-ner was finally ready.

But the masked gunmen got to me first—four of them, armed with AK-47s, a silenced Sterling machine pistol, and a Tariq 9mm, the stan-dard-issue pistol for the Iraqi Army. The men rushed into my office with their weapons drawn. A knowledge of Arabic wasn't necessary. "Come with us or we will kill you," one of the men said in clear English.

My instinct was to grab the 9mm pistol within arm's reach on my desk. It had one round in the chamber, ready to fire, and fifteen rounds in the magazine. An MP5 machine gun was in a file cabinet behind me; it was not within arm's reach.

Shoot it out—that's the training I received. If you are ever in a kidnapping situation, shoot it out, don't get caught, and don't get taken alive. Good advice, I suppose. I could have easily killed one of the men but not all of them, and they would have gunned me down within moments.

It was a split-second decision. I decided to live.

I signaled my decision by standing up slowly and allowing the kidnappers to walk me through the door and into the hallway.

I didn't know who these Arab men were or why they were after me. There were several possibilities to consider. Perhaps they were just one of the Mafia-like criminal gangs roaming the war-torn country and kidnapping wealthy Iraqis for ransom. A (much worse) possibility I didn't want to consider was that these men were part of the insurgent terrorist cell led by the ferocious Abu Musab al-Zarqawi. A notorious terrorist known to have links with Al-Qaeda, Zarqawi and his thugs were abducting and beheading their hostages in 2004, then releasing scenes of their gruesome murders on videotapes that were aired on the Internet and Al Jazeera television, an Arab-language news network. My best hope was that these armed-and-masked thugs, who looked to be in their twenties and thirties, were Iraqi "businessmen" who kidnapped for a living.

Hope is not a sound strategy, but it was all I had.

The man holding the Tariq pistol raised it to my head and ordered me to follow him downstairs. We passed by the closed office door of another American employee; then we turned right and went down about a dozen steps in the stairwell. When we got to the first floor, I was pushed into the hallway on my right and ordered to lie facedown on the floor.

Once downstairs, I saw that more than twenty masked and armed men had overrun the office. Majid was with them. He wasn't wearing a mask and was not even trying to hide from view. In fact, he was very busy helping some of the gang members as they looted the main office and ripped through file cabinets.

Majid was a traitor, all right. He had unlocked the iron security gate and quietly led the gang into our building. They walked right through the main door and into the front office without a fight.

Some of the gang members started to carry computers outside. A few of the men went back upstairs to my office, but for some reason, they didn't take my computer.

With Majid's inside help, the gang had caught our security men off guard while they were cooking their dinner in the kitchen at the rear of the building. From the hall, I could see the guards were also lying face-down on the floor underneath the dining table. Their arms were pinned behind their backs, and their wrists were bound with nylon handcuffs that looked something like large strap twist ties. I noticed they were similar to the ones carried on commercial airplanes to detain drunken passengers or would-be hijackers.

The guards had not made any noise, as the gang quickly took control of the first floor of the office building. I wondered why the guards had done nothing to protect us; why they didn't warn us we were under attack. If the guards had fired their weapons at the intruders, signaling an attack, I would have had time to grab my machine gun. My American colleague, Alex Loggins, was in his office right next door to mine, and he was also armed. Together, firing from the top of the stairwell, we might have been able to defend ourselves against these hoodlums.

That's when I realized that Alex wasn't downstairs with me; he was probably still back upstairs in his office, hiding behind a closed and pre-sumably locked door. I guess the kidnappers had only taken me because my door was open; they had ignored the closed door that concealed Alex, probably thinking it led to a closet.

And now I was downstairs, unarmed and unaided, surrounded by armed men who were either dressed in traditional Arab robes or wearing dark, cotton jogging suits. All of them wore masks—except the traitor.

The man with the Tariq pistol who had shoved me to the floor suddenly yanked my arms behind my back and strapped my hands together with the nylon tie cuffs. He asked me if I spoke Arabic.

"No," I replied honestly. "I only speak English."

"Is there anyone else upstairs?" the gunman asked.

"No," I lied. "I was the only one."

He seemed satisfied by my answer and helped me to my feet; then he and the armed men began moving their hostages out of the office building. Altogether there were six captives: myself; three Iraqis, whom I would never see again; a Filipino man named Robert Tarongoy, who would remain quietly by my side throughout most of my ordeal; and our "tea boy," who was from Nepal. (He was the employee who served us hot tea every day, but to his misfortune, he was not serving at the dinner party that night.)

We were shoved into the kitchen, past the stove, where the guards' food was still cooking, outside through a secondary doorway, and onto the front patio, where the iron gate gave access to the street. *All I have to do is stay alive*, I told myself. *The longer I can, the better it will be for my family.*

I was sure I would be killed; if I lived even until the end of the week, I was certain that would be a miracle. But a week would be good for my family, I thought. At least that would give them time to find out what had happened to me; to adjust to the fact of my kidnapping; to mentally prepare for my eventual death.

But first, they would have to come to terms with a little misconception on my part—I never told them that I had been transferred from Saudi Arabia to Baghdad. I didn't want my family and friends to worry about me working in a war zone, so I simply did not tell them. For all they knew, I was still working in Saudi Arabia, where the company's headquarters was located.

Although my wife, Susan, and I had divorced the previous year after thirty years of marriage, we remained good friends. She was living in

California, where she had just bought a new house, and I was still making payments to her under the divorce settlement, which helped her pay the mortgage. My oldest daughter, Carrie, and her husband, Rob, also lived in California, where Carrie worked as a family therapist and was helping children with autism. My youngest daughter, Amanda, was back in my hometown of Memphis with her little girl, my beautiful granddaughter, Sabrina, who was just eight years old.

I was, and still am, extremely loyal to my family. However, as I thought about them over the weeks and months ahead, I also had occasion to be grateful that I didn't have any pictures or letters from my family in my office, and that the black gym bag there, which contained every piece of information regarding who I was and where I came from, was dismissed as worthless and left behind by my kidnappers. All of my identification—driver's license, passport, and my retired military ID—was in that bag, folded inside a tan, walletlike pack that was on a long, cloth strap, so I could wear it around my neck when traveling to the U.S. Embassy and military bases throughout Baghdad. Ironically, the identification pack had a small American flag embroidered just beneath a zipper that held my cash, and beside the flag, stitched in dark brown, were the words *Iraqi Freedom*. The front of the pack showed my United States Defense Department uniformed service card, which identified me as a contractor—a Geneva Convention card for civilians accompanying the armed forces. Next to it was my Baghdad embassy identification card. When the pack was opened, it showed my Saudi Arabia Trading Company contractor card, as well as my weapons permit.

All of the ID cards bore various pictures of me; I had just turned fifty-six on June 23, and the photos revealed that my age was beginning to show. My hair was still dark brown, but the gray had mostly taken over my short-cropped beard and moustache. Blue eyes in some of the pictures looked through prescription glasses, which I had worn nearly all of my life.

The identification packed inside the duffel bag was locked away in the cabinet across from my desk, ready in case I ever had to make a hasty exit from Baghdad. Thank God, my kidnappers didn't ask me to get my things, and they didn't take the packed bag. For one thing, it would have meant certain death for me if they had discovered my retired military ID card, proof I had connections to the American military.

I joined the service in 1972 doing mostly logistics and government contracting, but I also had a security clearance and spent the first few years working in intelligence at the Pentagon with the Naval Security Group. After my retirement from the United States Navy, I went to work for the Royal Saudi Naval Forces in Jubail, Saudi Arabia, supporting the Saudi Eastern Fleet on the Persian Gulf, and I started working for the Saudi Arabia Trading Company in March 2004.

It was difficult to leave my family behind in the States, but Navy families get used to long separations. I still had a lot of good years in me, and the job in Iraq was a great opportunity to make a lot of money for my family and a more comfortable retirement for myself once I did finally pack it in and head back home to Memphis. I knew it would be hazardous work, but that was why the pay was so good, as my captors could attest.

Also tucked inside my identification pack was eight thousand dollars in cash. There were no banks operating in Baghdad, so I had to carry the money with me at all times. This was money I had saved for a Thanksgiving vacation back home—a stop in Memphis to see Amanda and my granddaughter, plus a visit with my sister, Barbara. Then I would fly to California to see Carrie and her husband. Maybe I would also stop in and see Susan and check out her new house.

Though the gang who took me captive never did learn anything about my family or me that day, they did take the vacation cash. So much for my vacation—I spent the next 311 days in captivity, virtually buried alive.

2

SHOOT-OUT AT THE COMPOUND

Alex had heard the commotion in my office and the gunmen taking me captive, and had waited behind his locked office door for an opportunity to alert my colleagues at the dinner party about the attack. But as the armed bullies pushed me outside and toward the front gate, where a caravan of Chevy Impalas, Toyota trucks, and Camry sedans had surrounded our compound, I heard gunfire erupt from inside the office building. At first I was afraid that the kidnappers had found Alex and that the shooting signaled his death, but as soon as Alex thought the coast was clear on the second floor, he burst out of his office, with a rain of cover fire from his Glock 9mm pistol, and ran to the doorway leading to the roof. Once there, he leaned over a concrete wall and fired down on the now scattering gang members. One of the kidnappers in the front courtyard, who, as it turned out, was not a skilled marksman, responded with rapid fire from his AK-47. He didn't aim the weapon at the roof; he just fired wildly into the air in all directions.

I was certain that my boss and the other guests at the party heard the shots fired by Alex and the returning fire, but gunshots in Baghdad were not uncommon: it could mean trouble—or signal a wedding or other cele-bration. Knowing this, Alex ran across the rooftop and bounded over the metal bridge to the other rooftop and down the stairs where the party was being held, so he could tell my boss about the attack.

Almost everyone in Iraq owns guns, and the Iraqi businessmen in attendance were no exception. The only problem was, they'd all left their AK-47s in their cars, which were parked in the front courtyard—where a major gun battle was about to erupt.

Meanwhile, the house across the street from the compound, where I lived with Zein and a British citizen named Mike Page, was loaded with weapons: AK-47s, an MP5, 9mm pistols, 12-gauge shotguns, tons of ammunition, even hand grenades. Earlier that year, Zein and I had checked out of a hotel after terrorists started bombing hotels where for-eigners were staying. The last straw for us was after a suicide bomber drove his van into a hotel lobby about four blocks from our hotel, killing several guests. After that attack, we moved into Mike's house. This was a relatively safer part of the city, so we thought we would be more secure. All of the houses and our office in our neighborhood are two stories and are constructed out of concrete blocks with steel bars across the win-dows. Concrete walls with a steel gate surround the houses, and while many of our colleagues also hired their own personal Iraqi guards for extra security in their homes, we did not. We'd heard far too many stories about guards being bribed by gang members to allow them access into homes so they could kidnap their residents. We didn't trust the private guards and instead armed our home and ourselves heavily. Unfortunately, most of the arms were *over there*, and I was not.

At the dinner party, though, Zein was carrying his Walther P-99 9mm pistol and the 9mm MP5 machine gun. Mike was there as well, packed with his MP5, a German-designed 9mm submachine gun. After the attack, Zein and Mike took the rooftop maze back to the office, aimed their weapons over the four-foot-high concrete wall, and opened fire on the gang as they carried computers and other equipment out of the office. Zein later said he did not see me and was not sure if I had already been taken hostage or if I was still in the office. Actually, four of the kidnappers and I were pinned down by their gunfire between the concrete wall, cut off from the awaiting getaway vehicles.

Now, the gang members in the courtyard dropped their loot and responded with heavy machine gun fire toward the roof, forcing Mike and Zein to hit the deck while bullets zoomed over their heads and penetrated the concrete walls that surrounded them.

When the machine guns briefly silenced from the street below, Mike and Zein stood back up and began firing at the kidnappers again, but they did not see that one of the gang members had slipped back into the office and was headed their way. The punk burst through the roof door, surprising both men, then pointed his AK-47 at Mike's chest.

The AK-47 is practically indestructible and can fire under the most abusive situations or lack of maintenance. The weapon operates just as effectively in the extreme heat of the desert as in the frozen tundra of Russia. Even if it's contaminated with dust or mud, the AK-47 will continue to fire. The Iraqi version of the venerable AK-47, the Tabuk Sniper Rifle, is a bastardized version of the Russian-designed assault weapon, with one long bolt to hold the stock on, as opposed to two screws. It's a good way to keep the wooden stock from breaking when it's bashed against someone's head.

Unless, that is, the weapon happens to be loaded with faulty ammunition.

Mike thought he was a goner, but when the thug pulled the trigger, the weapon jammed. Zein didn't hesitate; with thirty rounds in the clip, he deposited fifteen bullets into the gangster, who died on the spot. A pair of nylon handcuffs slipped from his hand into a pool of blood, along with a cell phone, a key piece of evidence that would later provide crucial clues that would lead to my eventual rescue.

Mike and Zein turned their attention back to the shooters in the courtyard and began firing again. By then, the gunmen had had just enough time to push me into a green Toyota Camry. As they drove away, the gang threw two hand grenades over the concrete wall in a last-ditch effort to kill Zein and Mike. Luckily for them, both of the hand grenades were duds, and neither exploded.

I was now surrounded inside the vehicle by four of the kidnappers, and the entire caravan of vehicles used for the attack began to move down the street. The man sitting on my right pulled off my prescription eyeglasses and threw them out the window, then pulled a black wool ski mask over my head and turned it around backwards, to act as a blindfold so I could not see where we were going. He then thrust my head down onto his lap so I could not be seen from outside of the vehicle. He stunk, badly. He obviously had not bathed in days. He began beating me on the head with his 9mm pistol. Over and over, he said that if I moved or made any noise, he would kill me. I was terrified. I was certain he was going to kill me right then and there and toss my lifeless body onto the side of the street.

The entire kidnapping operation was over in a matter of minutes. When the Iraqi police and American Army arrived just five minutes later, they found the compound littered with more than four hundred shells and the two dud hand grenades, the corpse of one of our guards who was killed in the attack, and one dead kidnapper.

3

CAPTIVE

As the Toyota raced down the street, I felt the driver forcing the vehicle over a median, turning it onto one of the numerous narrow streets that crisscross the main thoroughfare at various angles. The medians are meant to keep traffic on the correct side of the road, but in this war-ravaged city, it was common for Iraqis to drive on the wrong side of the highway or even on the sidewalks if necessary to get where they wanted to go. Therefore, any wild car ride through the streets of Baghdad probably wasn't going to attract that much attention.

I was trying to keep track of where we were headed, but for all I knew we could have actually been on the sidewalk. The car was so low to the ground it scraped bottom as it ran over numerous curbs. The kidnappers had threatened to kill me if I moved, but the car was bouncing around, and it knocked me back and forth between my kidnappers. It seemed like an impossible task, but I guess I stayed still enough—they didn't shoot me.

The windows were rolled up, so it was hot and stuffy inside the car, and it stank; whether it was body odor from the four men jammed in with me or a lingering aroma from the car itself, I didn't know, and frankly, I didn't have much time to think about it.

The wild ride only lasted about five minutes before we reached what turned out to be the first of many buildings the kidnappers used as safe houses for themselves and, this time, for me. The trip was so short I thought we could not be too far from my office. There had been a lot of twists and turns, but I believed we were probably still inside the Mansour district.

When we finally came to a stop, I could hear the creaking of a metal gate opening, then felt the car spin around and back up. More than likely, the house had a courtyard that was surrounded by a high concrete wall—standard architecture in Iraq. I heard the metal gate slam shut.

My feet were not bound, so the men pulled me out of the vehicle and into a house, where I was led up a spiral staircase that was no easy task to climb with my eyes covered and my hands tied behind my back. Then they took me up a second set of stairs to the third floor; I was shoved into a room and thrown facedown onto a hard, concrete floor.

I heard the door being locked and footsteps going downstairs, but I quickly realized at least two of my captors were still there, left behind to guard me. They started talking to one another in their native tongue, so I didn't understand a word. I was terrified and did not dare move, but at least the floor was cool—a nice reprieve from the hot, dusty car ride—and not nearly as smelly. And for a moment, I had a chance to think and try to assess my situation.

I could feel the nylon zip ties that were tied around my wrists cutting into my skin and figured I was probably oozing blood. With my elbows pulled behind my back, it increased the pressure and worsened the pain.

I was wearing military-style boots that laced up above my ankles by about ten inches, with a knife clipped inside the top of my right boot. It was a folding knife with a titanium blade, a potent weapon. Unfortunately, for the moment, it was completely useless; I doubted I could even get hold of it. I was pretty sure those two guards were mainly in the room to watch me and make sure I didn't try to escape. With the ski mask covering my face and eyes, and my hands bound tightly behind my back, it would have been suicidal to try and reach for the knife.

About twenty minutes later, other men came back into the room and started to search me. First they went through my pants pockets; then they rolled me over onto my back. I could feel the wetness of my shirt cuffs and knew my bound wrists were bleeding. I thought it was odd that they didn't strip me or take off my boots at that point. I was expecting my knife to be found at any moment and had what turned out to be short-lived relief that it wasn't found. For the time being, I could take comfort in still being armed.

Later, when I found out how these guys operated, I realized that this first search was to find some identification. My kidnapping was just an accident of my having been in the office when they raided it—they didn't actually know who I was or what I did for the company when they snatched me. My situation turned out to be the classic case of being in the wrong place at the wrong time. Once they identified who I was and my role at the company, they would figure out how much money they would demand for ransom.

I didn't like to contemplate the other tactic kidnappers were using at that time in Iraq. I hoped they wouldn't decide to just cut off my head and videotape the occasion for mass distribution to the international media—an opportunity for them to declare a victory for Al-Qaeda in Iraq.

The kidnappers grew frustrated after they searched me, and stormed out of the room and back downstairs. I could hear them shouting in Arabic for the next hour or so and guessed my fate was being discussed. Then they came back up to my room.

They took off my boots, and out came the knife. I was also stripped of everything else on me: a black leather belt that had been a gift from my daughter, Amanda, my clothes—black jeans and a gray Polo shirt, a gift from my sister—but what caused the most excitement from the bunch was my watch, a twelve-dollar Rolex rip-off that they jabbered about for several minutes as they passed it back and forth for examination. I could tell they thought it was real.

I didn't bother to tell them it was a fake, of course. A small victory for me.

After they took off my clothes, they gave me a cotton jogging suit to put on and asked me if I wanted to go to the bathroom. Actually, I had wanted to do that for quite some time but was afraid to ask. I said yes, and they led me into an adjoining bathroom. I was still blindfolded, but when they sat me down, I realized it was actually a Western-style, modern toilet, not just a hole in the floor that was the common household facility throughout Iraq. An actual commode was very unusual, and it made me wonder who in the world these people were.

The men stood there while I did my business, and I mulled over the significance of the toilet. Whoever owned this house had to be a wealthy businessman or, at the very least, a well-connected Iraqi. Indoor plumbing wasn't available to the average Mohammad in Iraq; many homes still had outhouses. The owner of this home was probably Sunni, an orthodox Muslim—the same religion of the former president of Iraq, Saddam Hussein, who had been captured the year before my ordeal began. It was usually the Sunnis who were wealthy in Iraq.

My hands were still tied behind my back, and my eyes were still blindfolded, so I was in no position to handle personal hygiene, which is dealt with very differently in Iraq. Most people in Iraq use their left hands to actually wipe themselves and then rinse their hands with water to clean them. (That's why it is considered an insufferable insult to use your left hand to offer something to someone in the Middle East.) Let's just say I wasn't able to clean up afterward.

The men shoved me back into the room and onto the floor, and again told me that if I moved or made any noise at all, they would kill me. Up to this point, I'd thought I was the only person in the room except for the guards. Now I realized someone else was there. I was pretty sure it was Robert, my Filipino colleague, whom I had seen being herded out of our office compound when I was taken. I had noticed four others being captured as well. Where were they? I wondered.

Robert, apparently, was already in the room when I first arrived. He must have been in a different car that got to this hideout ahead of me.

After my bathroom trip, the two men left behind to guard us stopped talking for a while, and things got quiet. Now I could hear Robert. He was near me, probably on the floor, too, softly crying and moaning. It gave me some comfort to know he was there—that someone I knew was there with me—but I thought it was probably best if I didn't try to talk to him right now. He obviously would have known I was there—heard them searching me, taking my clothes, asking me in English if I wanted to go to the bathroom—but he had said nothing. Maybe he was afraid to. Or perhaps he was gagged and wasn't able to speak.

I lay there in silence, wondering if Robert had been injured. He was still moaning. Had he been tortured? Would I be tortured? Would I live? And for how long?

I finally fell asleep there on the floor, my wrists bound behind me, my head covered, dressed in those thin, cotton clothes, wondering if anyone was looking for me.

••••

It only took about five minutes for the Iraqi police and the American army in military Humvees to arrive at the compound after the attack.

The kidnappers had been fast and, for the most part, thorough. They had pillaged the office. Computers and other equipment were taken, as well as my eight thousand dollars in cash. Of course, the army didn't know that was missing; I was the only one who knew about the stash I'd been saving for my vacation back home. As I said, the kidnappers had missed the tan cloth wallet pack holding my ID cards—it was still on my desk next to my computer—but all of the cabinets had been opened and looted.

The Army officials warned Zein and the others that they should not stay in Mansour that night. They were directed to go to the Green Zone about three miles away for protection.

In the meantime, within four hours of my capture, American officials notified my sister that I had been kidnapped.

4

THE FAMILY IS NOTIFIED

My daughter, Carrie, was folding clothes in her living room when the phone rang. It was my sister, Barbara, who had just been contacted by the State Department and informed of my kidnapping.

Barbara told her to sit down, but Carrie ignored her and kept working. However, my sister was insistent and told Carrie she had some bad news.

"What are you talking about? Dad's not even in Iraq; he's in Saudi Arabia," Carrie insisted.

Barbara did not know a lot of the details, so she told Carrie she needed to get off the phone quickly because the State Department said they would be calling my children to deliver the bad news. Carrie later told me that it was at least one hour before she was contacted by the State Department.

"She [the State Department employee] was very matter-of-fact; she just said, 'Your father was taken hostage,'" Carrie said. "I wanted some evidence; I was still in denial. I mean, how did they *know* it was my dad?

He was supposed to be in Saudi Arabia." She went on, "I asked her if she had any proof, and she told me that someone who knew my dad saw him being taken hostage."

As soon as Carrie hung up, she called her mother.

"I was cooking dinner when Carrie called. She was hysterically screaming; I had never heard her sound like that before," Susan later said. "She and her husband had only been married a couple of years, and I thought maybe something was wrong, maybe they had a fight.

"'Mom, Mom, they've taken Dad,' and she's screaming that they have taken him in a rock," Susan said. "It took a few moments for me to realize Carrie wasn't saying 'a rock,' but 'Iraq.'

"I thought he was in Saudi Arabia, but I took the phone number Carrie gave me, because I wanted to know why someone would do that, who would call Carrie and say such things," Susan told me. "I called the number, and sure enough, it was the State Department back in Washington, but they were closed for the day. That's when I first thought this could be real. But after a few minutes, I thought, *Naw, this is a mistake*. But just in case, I turned on the television to CNN."

Susan watched for any mention of the kidnapping, but the only news being reported that night was of the election between President Bush and Senator John Kerry, held the day after I was kidnapped. But while the news commentators never mentioned the attack on the compound earlier that day, the ticker tape of the day's headlines scrolling the bottom of the screen did: *An American contractor is being held hostage in Iraq*, it read.

Susan still did not believe it was me.

"That was someone else who was kidnapped in Iraq," Susan had reassured Carrie. "This has been some sort of mistake; it will all be okay."

And then, at 9:00 p.m., there was a knock on Susan's door.

"I thought it was Carrie, because she told me she was coming over to my house, but when I answered the door, it was a man and a woman dressed in black. They asked me if I was Susan Hallums, and then they told me my husband had been taken hostage in Iraq," Susan said.

"This is a mistake," she told them, but the FBI agents were insistent, and she finally let them into the house. Carrie arrived at Susan's house shortly afterward.

After detailing what little they knew at the time, the FBI agents managed to convince Susan that I was one of the six people taken from the office. What they wanted from her was some background information on me, any details they could use to identify me if the kidnappers called for ransom. For example, they wanted to know the name of the first dog I owned, my nickname as a youngster (Rusty), the name of my best friend in high school (Rick).

Although Susan and I had been divorced about two years by that point, we had been married thirty years and had remained friends. Even so, Susan was surprised the first visit from the FBI was to her and not my daughters. "I didn't understand why the FBI came to my house; Roy and I had been divorced for some time," she said.

Carrie stayed at Susan's house for about three days, and nearly the whole time she was curled up with her knees to her chest, facing the back of the sofa.

"Carrie always adored her father. The news crushed her," Susan said.

Carrie was blaming herself for my situation. She didn't like my working in the dangerous Middle East and felt guilty for not talking me out of the job. She'd also had a dream, just days before the attack, that I had been kidnapped, and she told Susan about it. Susan dismissed Carrie's nightmare at the time, but she now pays a lot closer attention to Carrie's dreams.

"She was just an intern," Carrie said of the young female who accompanied the FBI agent to her mother's house that night. "They just said they did not have any information and asked us to check off the box on a piece of paper to acknowledge they had come to my mother's house to talk to us, like we were confirming a visit from the cable guy.

"They also asked if we wanted ongoing counseling," she added, "but we never got any. After the FBI left Mom's house, we were just left there to deal with it. We kept watching the news on television, but it was all campaign news. Every now and then the little news ticker at the bottom of the screen would say an American had been kidnapped in Iraq, but they never mentioned my dad's name.

"I didn't know what to do," Carrie said. "I just hung out at Mom's house. I'm not even sure I knew where my husband was. I just wanted to be with someone who understood how I was feeling." She continued, "I would go online and look for any kind of information I could find. It was surreal to know it was your dad who had been kidnapped, but no one else knew about it."

In fact, Susan, Carrie, Amanda, and Barbara were instructed to tell no one that I was being held hostage in Iraq. No extended family members or even our close friends were allowed to know what was happening, and they were directed not to contact the media. It would be more than a month before anyone in the press learned my name.

Families of civilian hostages aren't provided the same kind of support services the families of military people are. Said Susan, "Being a hostage family is horrible."

Amanda, twenty-seven, and Sabrina, eight, were at the library when my sister called Amanda's cell phone and told her to come home immediately.

"I saw dark clouds outside the window, which meant a big storm was coming, and I thought that was why Aunt Barbara wanted us to get home," Amanda said. "But when I got in the car, Mom called and said Dad had been taken hostage. I said no, not my daddy."

She continued, "When the FBI came to the house a few hours later, I sent Sabrina to her bedroom before the agents told me what happened. Aunt Barbara was there when they told me Dad had been kidnapped in Iraq. The news had sunk in for Aunt Barbara, but I just could not believe it, because Dad wasn't in Iraq; he was working in Saudi Arabia. Unfortunately, my little girl was eavesdropping in the hallway. I was a single mom at the time, and my dad, whom she affectionately called Dapa, was the main father figure in Sabrina's life."

The news was so traumatic for little Sabrina, it would give her nightmares for years to come. Amanda was in denial nearly the whole time.

"We were all hostages too," Amanda said. "The uncertainty, the not knowing, day after day after day."

It would only get worse.

5

THE MOSQUE

I slept on the hard concrete floor that night, without even a thin, ragged blanket to keep my feet warm. My captors had taken my boots and socks and left me hog-tied, and with the night temperatures dipping below fifty degrees in November, I was cold and uncomfortable.

I woke up when I heard the kidnappers reciting their morning prayers. Muslims are supposed to pray five times a day: once before dawn, then another prayer around 11:00 a.m., again at 2:00 p.m., a fourth prayer just after sunset, and the final prayer of the day at 8:00 p.m. Prayer times change every day in one-minute increments; it's all based on the position of the sun. For the very conservative Wahhabi[1] gang that had kidnapped me, just keeping track of their prayer schedule could be a full-time job.

My kidnappers were particularly busy with their worship. They told me they prayed five times a day because they were good Muslims. I learned to be thankful for their devotion. By tracking these "good Muslims" saying their prayers, I was able to keep up with the time of day and the passing of days throughout my ordeal.

One of the men came into the room and pushed up the bottom of the ski mask just enough to allow me to take a drink of water. The mask was still covering my nose and eyes, but because it was made with a loose-knit material, I was at least able to breathe through it with some ease.

As soon as I took a sip, the guard yanked the mask back down over my mouth. I was told to lie back down and be quiet.

That's what I did for that entire day: lie on that concrete floor in complete silence. Not alone, of course; guards came and went, and I knew Robert was nearby. We still didn't dare to speak to one another. At least one guard was always present; anything we said aloud would be overheard, and I felt there might be some danger in that. Robert probably thought the same.

Robert suffered from severe headaches, for which he was supposed to take medication, but I doubted the kidnappers had brought along the pills when they took him and the rest of us hostage. I could hear him moan every now and then and suspected he was probably having a terrible headache.

In my solitude I spent a lot of time worrying about my family. I didn't know if they had been told that I'd been kidnapped, or if anyone had let them know what that might mean or what the kidnappers might intend to do with me. I was mostly troubled about how worried they would be. There was my sister: she had high blood pressure, and I was afraid that news of my kidnapping would be detrimental to her health.

And my children; I was concerned about the financial impact of my capture on the girls. If I was killed, I had life insurance through the company, but only for about $120,000—not all that much, really, to help out two daughters and a grandchild. Carrie and her husband were living in a house I owned in California. It was still mortgaged, and I sometimes had to help with the payments. What if they couldn't make them on their own and the bank foreclosed and they had to move out?

Next I worried for a while about losing my car and truck when the monthly payments stopped being paid. Then I worried about Susan and how she would make house payments without my spousal support checks. I finally decided that worrying wasn't accomplishing anything, and it was getting a little out of hand: here I was, tied up and blindfolded and being held hostage by terrorists somewhere in the middle of Iraq, and I was worrying about paying alimony!

Every now and then, the guards who stayed in the room with Robert and me would give us some water. At one point, I figured out that a window in the room was accounting for changes in brightness, barely discernible through my mask. As the light faded, I could tell that the sun was setting for the evening. My second night of captivity was approaching.

About two hours after the sun set, the gang members came for Robert and me. They led us down the first staircase and then the spiral stairs to the first floor, where we were forced to lie facedown on the ground. Several men were in the room, speaking in excited tones. I didn't understand the words, but I knew something was about to happen.

What? I wondered. *Torture? Death?* The only option that didn't seem likely was that they were about to untie my hands, remove my blindfold, and say, "Sorry, our mistake," and send me home.

The answer didn't come immediately. I was made to sit up on the floor, and one guy came up behind me. I could hear him pulling tape off a roll. Starting just under my left ear, he began wrapping the tape around my head. I still had the ski mask on, of course, but that didn't bother him. The tape was wound around about eight times right over the ski mask, mostly covering the area where my mouth was, presumably to prevent me from yelling for help if there was anyone around to hear me.

My feet were then bound, and I was carried out of the house and stuffed into the trunk of a car. I landed on a pile of tools and junk; Robert was tossed in on top of me.

The tape prevented us from talking, but even if we could, we still wouldn't have dared. We could hear the voices of two men in the backseat, which meant that they were also in a position to hear anything we might say.

The two of us—trussed, blindfolded, gagged, and sharing a bed of tools—made for a very uncomfortable ride, but after about ten minutes, the vehicle came to a stop.

I could hear Muslim prayers over a loudspeaker from a minaret, a prayer-summoning tower.

We were at a mosque. This did not bode well.

Mosques were off-limits to American forces. They were places of worship for Muslims, holy shrines to their religion. It was important that we respect the religion and avoid causing any incident that might be regarded as sacrilege. So if a rescue party had been assembled after the attack on the company compound, this is the one place where they would be forbidden to look for me.

Still bound and gagged, we were taken into the mosque.

Iraqi architecture almost always includes a walled courtyard. Nearly every mosque, home, or office is hidden behind high concrete or stucco walls. I had to assume that was the case here; otherwise, surely someone would notice and wonder about two men being pulled from the trunk of a car and carried into a mosque. Apparently the move went completely unnoticed.

Inside, we were taken to a small room; somewhere close by I could hear the sounds of an imam leading prayers. It sounded as if a large group of men were attending the service that evening, and they were delivering the appropriate responses aloud.

Since it was still the month of Ramadan, I contemplated whether murder was in the works, and if they were going to carry out the deed right there in the mosque while recording it on videotape.

There was a reason I kept having recurring thoughts that my captors might be preparing to stage my demise for television audiences around the world. Earlier that year, on May 11, a video was posted on the Internet that showed the beheading of Nick Berg, a United States businessman.

The accompanying narrative said that Zarqawi had kidnapped Berg and that his death was necessary to avenge the abuse of Iraqi detainees at Abu Ghraib prison.

The video was barbaric. While the full thing was available on the Internet, no mainstream TV network had shown the actual beheading. They did show the lead-up to it, however, including this statement by the victim: "My name is Nick Berg; my father's name is Michael; my mother's name is Susan. I have a brother and sister, David and Sarah. I live in West Chester, Pennsylvania, near Philadelphia." I had seen the video, which showed several masked men surrounding Berg, who was dressed in a vivid orange jumpsuit. One of the captors read a statement. Then another one of the terrorists decapitated Berg with a knife. His screams could be heard while the men shouted, "*Allah Akbar!*" (God is great).

I couldn't bear to think about it. But there was one thing I knew I would do everything in my power to prevent: my captors would have to kill me before I would identify my children or anyone else in my family in a taped video. I decided I would provide as little information to my kidnappers as possible. If they wanted to know something, I would give a very short, one-word answer to protect my family. I don't know what lies those terrorists told Berg, or what torture he underwent, but from his experience I learned that nothing really mattered to them—they would kill you anyway.

But I had to quit thinking about death and start thinking about living. That turned my attention to my stomach; I had not eaten in forty-eight hours.

I was really craving a *shawarma*, an exotic pita sandwich considered the taco of the Middle East. Shawarma is Turkish for "turn," and the meat, whether it's chicken or lamb, is cooked on a giant rotisserie. Shawarmas are sold on the sidewalks of Iraq, usually in front of an indoor restaurant, by a man dressed as a chef. I mentally began to make one for myself. I decided on lamb instead of chicken, spiced with mace, cinnamon, garlic, cayenne pepper, and cumin. Then I'd top it with a tahini dressing made with yogurt, and I'd stuff in some chopped cucumbers and tomatoes, maybe even some french fries.

Thinking passed the time as I constructed the shawarma in my head. Unfortunately, it didn't fill my stomach, and the men who were holding us hostage in the mosque did not bring us any food that night, or water either. I spent my second night in captivity cold and hungry, sleeping on the floor, tape still covering my mouth, my ankles bound, and my arms tied behind my back. On the plus side, it did seem that the bleeding around my wrists had finally stopped.

But Robert was still having difficulties with his handcuffs and asked one of the guards to loosen it just a little.

"Shut up or we will kill you," the guard responded.

6

PRAYERS

Prayers filled the air in the mosque, a signal that dawn was approaching and that I had lived through the night.

Robert and I were in a small room next to the main hall where the congregation met for prayers. Did all the worshippers here know that two men were being kept prisoner, locked away, lying on a concrete floor all day and night, just a few feet away from them?

I felt that must be the case. Many mosques in Iraq were just what they seemed to be—Muslim houses of worship. Other mosques hid behind a facade of religion to serve as places where the members of hard-core extremist groups could meet, plot, and hide in total privacy. Or hide kidnap victims. Or carry out ritual murders.

In our situation there was too much going on for it to be a true mosque with no sinister purpose. Guards came in and out about every twenty minutes to check on us. Each time, they tested my mask to make sure it covered my face, then they pulled on the bindings on my hands and feet to make sure they were secure. When the guards were not in the room with us, they stood right outside our door, and we could hear them talking.

Robert was lying on the floor next to me, yet we did not say a word to each other all day. I figured if I could hear the guards talking, then they could certainly hear me whisper to Robert, so I didn't take any chances.

I knew we were close to the main hall because I could clearly hear the imam talking and leading the prayers throughout the day. I wondered what he was saying as he shouted to the all-male congregation and they shouted back. "We have American hostages in the next room; let's kill them!" perhaps. I tried not to visualize the men storming into the room, dressing Robert and me in orange jumpsuits, and carrying us into the main hall to be decapitated.

When I was sure the guards were not in the room, I brought my knees up to my face and managed to push the mask up just enough so that I could see underneath. Tilting my head back, I quickly scanned the room. Robert was across the room from me, lying on the floor and not moving; he might have even been asleep. There was nothing else in the room: no jumpsuits folded and waiting in readiness, certainly nothing in the color orange. I wanted to make sure of that.

I rubbed my face against my knees some more, trying to pull and stretch the fibers of the mask in the area where it covered my eyes so that I might be able to see through it. I fooled with it as long as I dared and then nudged it back into place over my eyes and mouth. I could see— not much and not too clearly, but it made me feel a little better.

After the final prayers were said for the day—I'd been keeping track, and I knew it must be 8:00 p.m.—I heard the sound of an engine, and shortly thereafter, the guards came for us. As they carried us out, I took some solace in the fact that we were being moved outside, to another location, and not into the main prayer hall to be killed on behalf of Al-Qaeda.

I could tell by the sounds coming from the vehicle that it had a large engine—probably a V-8, and most likely a Suburban, a popular vehicle in Iraq. Using my newly found vision through the ski mask, I could tell that it was white.

Robert was dumped on the floor of the backseat, and they laid me on top of the seat, facedown. All of a sudden, I could hear that someone was beating Robert and threatening him, and then I felt the pain of a 9mm pistol slamming against my own head. The death threats continued: if we moved, we died, one of the guards said.

I felt something soft falling on me, and now that I could see a little bit, I could tell that the kidnappers were hiding us by stacking bundles of blankets, still packaged in plastic bags, on top of us. I recognized the goods—cheap blankets made in China and common items for sale in the local Baghdad markets. Anyone who happened to glance into our vehicle would think the men were merchants on their way to the market. They would never be aware that Robert and I were underneath the load, sweating and having a hard time breathing in the heat from the vehicle and smothering underneath the weight of the blankets.

I heard the metal clanging of the mosque gate opening, and it sounded like there was another car ahead of us, probably leading the way to check for American army or Iraqi police checkpoints on the road to wherever we were heading. After the vehicle started moving and the blankets began to jostle a bit, I took the opportunity to move my head between the seat and the door to position myself so that I could breathe easier.

We drove for about two hours, but never in a direct route: the kidnappers made several U-turns and stops. Once again, I tried to keep some track of our route—tried to hear sounds and get some idea of where I was.

Many bridges in Iraq were bombed during the war and replaced with temporary metal ones. At one point, we crossed one of those temporary bridges, and I knew we were headed out of Baghdad, but I did not know in which direction.

The driver eventually turned off a paved road and onto what felt like a farm field. I bounced along with the blankets as we drove over the rough, plowed ground.

The Suburban eventually came to a stop. Some of the men got out of the vehicle and started talking to someone else, whose voice I had not heard before. Then there came the sound of another metal gate opening, and I figured we were entering another one of the ubiquitous compounds.

We were carried into the house and given a drink of water. I could vaguely see that we were in a small room, probably an extra bedroom, but there was no furniture in it. As the guards left us alone for the night, I heard them close the door, followed by the sound of a lock clicking into place.

It didn't take me long to figure out that I was somewhere near Fallujah, the most violent city in Iraq, located about forty miles northwest of Baghdad. The city was a hotbed of Sunni resistance, and now American marines, along with several Iraqi army battalions, were lined up on the other side of the Euphrates river, preparing for a massive attack that would become known as the Second Battle of Fallujah—the most pitched battle involving American forces since the Vietnam War.

Every night I was there, and sometimes during the day, I could hear the sounds of artillery shells flying overhead and hundreds of rounds of machine-gun fire. I didn't know if this was a good or bad thing for me. I hoped that it was the cavalry coming to the rescue, but seriously wondered if anyone could possibly know where I was and if the people doing the shooting had any idea that there was an American captive in their combat zone. I prayed I wasn't about to get caught in some deadly cross fire.

Once again, I was in the wrong place, and at the wrong time.

7

BREAKFAST AND BEATINGS

The next day, guards brought Robert and me some Arabic bread and cheese to eat and some tea to drink; it was the first time we had eaten in days.

But my comfort was short-lived. After we finished eating, one of the guards dragged me out of the small room into what was probably the living room and forced me to sit on the floor on my knees. Not only was the position uncomfortable; it was downright painful.

The black mask still covered my face, but I could see some light and detect movement. I could tell there were several men in the room. One man who acted as the leader began to question me in Arabic, while another man translated what he was saying to me in English.

"We know you are CIA," the translator said.

"I'm not CIA," I responded, "I am here to provide food for the people who are helping rebuild Iraq."

"We know you are CIA, and there is no need to lie about it," he said. "We are going to ask you some more questions, and if you lie, we will kill you.

"What is your name?" the translator asked me.

"Roy Hallums," I responded.

"Are you American?"

"Yes, I am."

They asked me what company I worked for, and what the company was doing in Iraq, and I answered them honestly. But then they asked me about my family. They wanted to know where my family was, if they were with me in Iraq, or back home in the States.

I didn't answer right away, and the translator told me that the gang had taken computers and other files from the office. The translator said they already knew everything about me and that if I lied to them, they would kill me. I didn't believe him. If they already knew everything about me, then why the questions? But I decided to be as truthful as possible; it wasn't worth risking death just to test them.

They didn't wait for me to answer their questions about my family; instead, they turned their attention back to my employment record.

"Where did you work before you came to Iraq?" the translator asked.

"I worked in Saudi Arabia for about ten years before I came to Iraq," I answered. I thought my response might please the kidnappers, and the fact that I was not a stranger to the Middle East and was working toward providing them a better lifestyle might bring me favor. But I was wrong. My answer just angered the gang leader, who shouted in Arabic at the translator.

"If you lived in Saudi Arabia for ten years, then you must speak Arabic!" the translator then shouted at me. "I demand that you start speaking Arabic directly to our leader."

I told him that although I had lived in Saudi Arabia for a long time, I could not speak Arabic.

This angered the leader, who was sitting to my left, and with his right hand he backhanded my head with his pistol and shouted in English for me to "speak Arabic!"

"I only know a few words of Arabic; I cannot carry on a conversation in Arabic," I pleaded in English.

The leader again started to pistol-whip me, then he shoved the barrel of the gun into my mouth.

"Start speaking Arabic right now, or I will kill you!" the leader said.

I could not say anything with the gun in my mouth, but as soon as he removed it, I told him that if I could speak Arabic, I would obviously start speaking it right now.

"You are a liar!" the leader screamed, and began thrashing my head again with his gun, nearly knocking me off my wobbly knees that had become numb with sleep.

After the men were satisfied that repeatedly slamming me upside the head with a pistol could not force me to speak Arabic, they began the interrogation again, using the English-speaking gang member to translate questions from the ringleader to me.

"What are the phone numbers for your office and your employer?" the translator asked.

This was not good. All of the phone numbers of my contacts in Iraq were saved on my cell phone, which was left behind in my office. I never bothered to memorize any of the numbers. The gang members did not sound pleased with my answer.

"Where are you from? Where does your family live?" he asked.

I told them I was from Memphis, Tennessee.

"What are the phone numbers for your family?" the translator demanded.

I told him I did not know any of my family's phone numbers back in the States off the top of my head, that all of those phone numbers were also saved on my cell phone.

The gang leader came forward again. By this time I had learned from hearing other gang members talking to him that his name was Omar, and Omar was angry, again.

Omar began beating me on the head, demanding in English that I give him the phone numbers. There were several moments when I felt as if I were in a cartoon: Omar hit me so hard I saw stars, and he wasn't even using his full strength. If he'd wanted to, he could have hit me hard enough to kill me, but he held back. Nonetheless, the beating was hard enough that at one point I nearly blacked out.

"I have treated you gently so far," Omar said after he was done beating me. "It will be very bad for you if you do not give me the phone numbers. I am going outside for fifteen minutes, and when I get back, it will be very bad for you if you do not give me these numbers."

Omar left the room and slammed the door. The men left behind to guard me talked quietly among themselves. I could not tell what they were saying, but I knew they were talking about Omar.

I didn't dare move, although I really wanted to, because I had lost most of the feeling in my legs. I'm not sure if I was bleeding, because I could not feel my face, but I could feel a searing pain in my temple that stretched across my forehead.

I considered what phone numbers I really had memorized. I knew my sister's number; it had not changed over the years. I could remember parts of Amanda's phone number in Memphis. But I did not know Susan's number at her new house, and Carrie had moved recently, so I was certain I did not know hers either.

After some time, Omar came back into the room and demanded the phone numbers.

"I really do not know their phone numbers," I responded, and I was telling the truth. "If I knew the numbers, I would give them to you."

"Liar!" Omar yelled, and he began pounding me again.

After about ten minutes he demanded the phone numbers again, and without waiting for me to answer, he jammed the gun back inside my mouth.

"Give me the phone numbers or I will kill you!"

I just shook my head no, and Omar beat me again.

At some point, I lost consciousness. When I awoke, Omar started questioning me again.

He wanted to know who my bosses were at the trading company, and how they could be taken hostage as well. Omar wanted to know how much money the owners had, what kind of cars they drove, how expensive their homes were.

When I told Omar that I did not know, that I had never been to their homes, he called me a liar, and the beatings started again. But then one of the other men said something in Arabic, and Omar stopped hitting me.

That's when Omar told me they were holding me for ransom, and because I was an American, they were asking for twelve million dollars for my release. I was surprised to hear that it was such a large amount; most kidnappers I had heard about in Iraq were demanding ransoms in the tens of thousands of dollars.

"No one will pay twelve million dollars for me," I told Omar.

"We will call the American Embassy, and they will bring the twelve million dollars; then we will let you go," Omar said.

These guys may have been efficient at kidnapping, but they had no clue about American policies against negotiating with terrorists or paying off kidnappers.

"No," I responded, "the Embassy will not pay for me."

"We have a cousin who is being held in Abu Ghraib prison. If we do not get the money, we will call the American Embassy and they will let our cousin go; then we will let you go," he said.

I said no, the Embassy will not do that either.

"Then we will contact the company, and they will bring the twelve million," Omar said.

"I work for a small company; they cannot raise twelve million dollars," I insisted.

"Then we will call your family, and they will bring us twelve million," Omar said.

At the mention of my family, I snapped.

"If my family had twelve million dollars, I would not be here, working in Iraq!"

Omar responded by slamming his gun against my head.

"No, no, we will call the American Embassy, and they will bring the money," Omar said.

At that, I knew I was going to be held captive for a very long time. Having lived in the Middle East, I knew negotiations are extremely slow on a good day, and it was going to be some time before the gang came to the realization that they were not going to get any money from my government. I was nervous about what the men might do when they finally figured this out.

"Are you diabetic?" Omar asked.

I considered telling him that I was, but was concerned they might actually force me to take insulin, which would be dangerous for someone who, in fact, is not diabetic.

"No," I said.

"Do you have high blood pressure?"

"Yes," I lied. I did not have high blood pressure. In fact, I was pretty healthy before I was taken captive, but I thought that by lying about my health, they might stop beating me, and I might get better treatment. Maybe they would treat me less harshly if they thought I had an illness that might cause them problems down the road.

"Yes," I repeated, "I have high blood pressure."

The trick worked. The men dragged me back into the small room and dropped me on the cold, concrete floor, then returned to the living room for their evening prayers.

I had a terrible headache that lasted for several days. Needless to say, Omar did not offer me any aspirin after our introductory meeting.

The beatings delivered by Omar left some tears in the ski mask, and I maneuvered it around my head to get a better view of the room in which I was being held. I could see Robert. He wasn't moving and was probably asleep. All of the walls in the room were painted a sort of army green color. Actually, it looked as though they had stolen a can of paint from the American Army to paint the walls.

I didn't get much sleep that night. I could hear gun battles, and at one point I thought I heard one of those small, remote-controlled observation planes deployed by the Marines. It sounded like a lawn mower, and the noise continued all night. I hoped it was the American forces and that they were looking for me. But I worried about what would happen if the house in which we were staying was actually hit by mortars or attacked by Army Special Forces. What if one of our guys dropped a bomb on another house that belonged to one of the kidnappers and killed his family? The gang would certainly avenge the family's death by killing me.

I prayed that the remote-controlled plane was searching for me. I prayed that the artillery fire did not hit the house where we were held. And I prayed for God to get me out of there.

8

THE KIDNAPPING BUSINESS

D an O'Shea, a reserve Navy SEAL lieutenant commander, served his final post–September 11 military duty in Iraq, assigned to the American Embassy and the FBI as an interagency liaison officer. On his first day on the job in July 2004, he was handed a kidnapping case of a Bulgarian civilian; the crisis quickly exploded with as many as forty kidnappings a month.

News reports of abductions like mine were the exception, as Americans represented only a fraction of the victims. Overwhelmingly, the kidnapping targets were local Iraqis and international workers who came to support the coalition's rebuilding efforts, contractors, truck drivers, Arab businessmen, aid workers, and journalists from around the world who were covering the ongoing war.

The United States military and FBI were not traditionally assigned to address kidnapping cases, so the responsibility fell to the American Embassy to answer the official requests for help that came pouring in from around the world. To address the growing crisis, O'Shea made a formal presentation to ambassador James Jeffrey, the deputy chief of mission, who sanctioned the formation of the Hostage Working Group.

The group's mission was "to advise, make recommendations to the ambassador on actions to deter, prevent, and be prepared to respond to hostage-taking incidents" and to "support resolving hostage-taking incidents through rapid, vetted information sharing, intelligence relay and coordination through diplomatic, military, intelligence and law enforcement channels." The Hostage Working Group had three simple priorities: to prevent kidnappings, recover hostages, and bring those responsible for the kidnappings to justice.

However, some actions by our international partners only inflamed the terrorists and encouraged more kidnapping, which, as I previously mentioned, had become Iraq's number one growth industry following the collapse of Saddam's government in 2003. As an example, after Sunni kidnappers snatched a Philippine citizen in July, the Philippines buckled quickly to their demands, setting a dangerous precedent. Angelo de la Cruz, who was working in Iraq as a truck driver, was released by his captors after his government agreed not only to pay the six million dollars in ransom, but also to pull Filipino troops out of the war in Iraq.

The Bush administration was not pleased and said that the Philippine government's decision to pull their fifty-one troops ahead of schedule sent the wrong signal to the terrorists. He was right.

"It was no surprise to anyone that another Filipino [Robert] was targeted a few months after Angelo was released," O'Shea later said. "We were also aware that companies were paying off ransoms for their employees, and we knew that ultimately this was putting money in the hands of the insurgents who were killing U.S. troops."

At the time of my capture, there were four groups of Sunni terrorists operating in Iraq who were kidnapping hostages: Al-Qaeda, the Islamic Army, the 1920 Revolution Brigade, and the Mujahideen Army. Al-Qaeda is ultimately led by Osama bin Laden, but in Iraq, where it was one of the most dangerous and violent extremist groups of all, it was led by al-Zarqawi, who was kidnapping and beheading Westerners and then distributing the gruesome videotapes to the public.

The Islamic Army in Iraq was a hard-core group that often worked in concert with Al-Qaeda, but later split with the group over significant issues. Specifically, Al-Qaeda started murdering members of the Islamic Army in 2006 after al-Zarqawi was killed in an air strike north of Baghdad.

The 1920 Revolution Brigade, a nationalist Sunni group, was made up mostly of members from Saddam's disbanded army, who also (after my release) turned against Al-Qaeda and began cooperating with U.S. forces because the Al-Qaeda terrorists were also targeting its local tribes for violence.

But it was the Jaish al-Mujahideen (Mujahideen Army), the most ruthless and brutal thugs native to Iraq, who had taken me hostage. These were former intelligence officers in the Fedayeen Saddam (Saddam's Men of Sacrifice)—his mafia soldiers, if you will. During Saddam's twenty-plus–year reign of terror, more than one million of his subjects disappeared, never to be seen again. That was the work of the Fedayeen Saddam. It was the cruel acts of these paramilitary assassination squads that got Saddam convicted of genocide and later sentenced to death. Under the direction of Saddam's eldest son and heir apparent, Uday, as many as fifty Iraqis a day were kidnapped and probably killed after enduring extreme torture. Saddam's "Men of Sacrifice" were essentially hoodlums, highly trained kidnappers who were skilled in the tactics of hostage-taking, an accepted part of life in Iraq.

Kidnapping was a legitimate business; it is in the Koran. And now I was literally a part of the economy. As Dan O'Shea later ascertained, my abduction (and the abductions of hundreds of others) was, in fact, funding the insurgency in Iraq to fight against my own countrymen. As hundreds of millions of dollars in ransoms were paid, the kidnappers kept their take, and the rest of the money went to their cause: forcing the Americans out of Iraq—or killing them.

"Kidnapping was a booming industry in Iraq in 2004," O'Shea said. "That was my challenge. They [Sunni kidnappers] all wanted the same things and shared the same vision—they wanted to throw out the invaders and used hostage-taking to spread fear, raise funding for the insurgency, discredit the U.S.-led coalition, and to intimidate those who worked for the new government." He went on, "Kidnapping was an effective tool and terrorist weapon of mass effect."

The day after I was kidnapped, Al Jazeera aired a videotape of Margaret Hassan, the director of CARE International's operations in Iraq, who had been kidnapped on October 19. She was called the Mother Teresa of Baghdad for her charity outreach to the city's most impoverished. This Irish woman, who had dual citizenship in Iraq, was shown pleading for her life, fainting, and having water thrown on her by her captors. (Only a portion of the tape was played on the air by Al Jazeera, which deemed it too graphic to show in its entirety.) The kidnappers were threatening to sell her to Al-Qaeda unless British prime minister Tony Blair withdrew troops from Iraq. The body of a woman found November 15 by American troops in Fallujah was originally believed to be Hassan (her arms and legs had been chopped off and her throat slit). Later, a video of Hassan's execution surfaced on a jihadist Web site, but Margaret's body was never recovered.

Our kidnappers' demands were different for us than they were for Hassan. They wanted ten million dollars for Robert, and twelve million dollars for me. In total, they were demanding that my company, a Muslim-owned business, turn over twenty-two million dollars for our safe release. At some point in their negotiations, they also demanded the release of four prisoners being held at the Abu Ghraib prison.

In many cases, the Hostage Working Group found out about kidnappings after the media reported it. In my case, though, my name was not made public in any news reports of the attack on the compound. The FBI wanted to keep my identity secret so they could make every effort to rescue me. They especially did not want information about my being in the military to get out. In the media I was simply "an American."

Reuters reported on November 1 that "gunmen kidnapped an American, a Nepali, and two Arabs . . . 'They stormed the villa with automatic rifles and rocket-propelled grenades,' said a police source. 'They had no chance.'"[1]

On November 2, BBC News pointed out that two Americans, Eugene Armstrong and Jack Hensley, as well as a British citizen named Kenneth Bigley, had been kidnapped from the same once relatively safe district of Mansour in September. "All three men were killed."[2] Under Zarqawi, Al-Qaeda in Iraq had beheaded the men. And just two days after we were kidnapped, armed gunmen kidnapped another American, a contractor for the army.

Conflicting reports continued as to how many Iraqis were kidnapped during my ordeal. I was told later that it was, in fact, three Iraqi guards who were kidnapped, but they were released hours later and found blindfolded and handcuffed in the Hay al-Amil area of Baghdad. I never did learn if ransoms had been paid for their release.

Agence France-Presse (AFP) got the account right on November 1: "A US citizen, an Asian, and four Iraqis working for a Saudi company were kidnapped at gunpoint from their offices in Baghdad on Monday, officials said, adding to a swollen cast of hostages in Iraq." The story continued, "Outgunned on the ground, militants in Iraq use foreign hostages as weapons in a bid to fight off the US-led military coalition and undermine the interim government."[3]

When my family watched the evening news that night on CBS, Dan Rather informed viewers that the biggest problem facing the winner of the upcoming presidential election would be what to do about Iraq. "There were more bombings and ambushes there today," he said, "and a raid in suburban Baghdad by kidnappers, who took an American civilian and three other people hostage."[4] The report that followed (by Elizabeth Palmer in Baghdad) included the tidbit that, before storming our office, the attackers had warned bystanders to get inside or they'd be killed.

The next morning, November 2, the headline in the *New York Times* read, "The 2004 Campaign: Insurgency; American Is Among 4 Captives Seized in Baghdad Kidnapping." "The American was not identified, and by early Tuesday, no one had claimed responsibility for the kidnapping," the reporters wrote.[5]

Also that day, the Associated Press reported that our guards had already been released, and although American Embassy officials were still withholding my name, word had leaked out to reporter Mariam Fam that Roberto Tarongoy, an accountant, was one of the kidnap victims. "More than 160 foreigners have been abducted this year by militants with political demands or by criminals seeking ransom. At least 33 captives have been killed," Fam reported, adding, "The abduction came two days after authorities found the decapitated body of another hostage [wrapped in an American flag], 24-year-old Japanese backpacker Shosei Koda. Al-Zarqawi's Al-Qaeda in Iraq group said it had kidnapped Koda and demanded a withdrawal of Japanese troops from the country."[6]

At the time of my kidnapping, Zarqawi had six kidnappings/ beheadings to his credit. So Dan O'Shea assumed the worst: that it was this same beast who had ordered the attack on my office (and our subsequent kidnappings). As CNN pointed out in its account of my abduction, "the city remains home to a terror network run by Abu Musab al-Zarqawi, a Jordanian militant who has sworn allegiance to Osama bin Laden."[7] "Meanwhile," the AFP reported, "expectations mounted for an all-out assault on the rebel-held city of Fallujah, west of Baghdad."[8] American troops had already begun bombing and shelling over Fallujah on October 29, before I was kidnapped. The mortars continued until the Second Battle of Fallujah officially erupted on November 8.

9

ALLAH AKBAR!

It was Thursday, November 4, and the house was quiet all day. I didn't even hear the guards except when they brought meals for Robert and me. It wasn't much, just some stale rice, flat pita bread, and water. At one point they gave me some kind of soup. But it was food, a sign that they wanted to keep us alive, if only for a little while.

The guards had untied our hands from behind our backs and retied them in front of our stomachs so we could eat—and thankfully, they did not retie our hands behind our backs after we were finished.

I pulled my mask up from over my mouth and nose to eat, and for the first time I could see the damage that the plastic ties were doing to my wrists. The strips were cutting into my flesh, and I was bleeding, causing me great concern that I would get an infection. If I did become infected from the dirt and grime gathered along the cuts, I doubted that the guards were going to provide any sort of medical treatment. So I poured a little bit of the water I'd been given over my wrists to rinse off the blood and dirt. The last thing I needed was to get gangrene. I was already starting to lose feeling in my hands, and my fingers could barely move.

I could not hear any guards talking, so I used the opportunity to push my mask up so I could sneak a peek around the room. Robert was sitting on the other side of the bare room; his mask was pulled down just below his nose, and he ate while blindfolded.

I hadn't been imagining the horrible color of the walls the previous night. Earlier, I called it "army green"; in actuality, it was like puke green, a very odd color to cover four walls. There were no windows in the room, no chance of escape except through the front door, and I had no idea where the guards were.

But what if I could make it out of the house? I wasn't even sure of where I was in Iraq at the time, but judging by the distances we had driven and the sounds of battle the night before, we were most likely in Fallujah. I imagined myself standing on the side of a road, winding through the desert of Iraq, with my thumb sticking out to hitch a ride with some traveling Iraqi.

Maybe not.

My situation seemed hopeless. Even if I managed to escape and make contact with another Iraqi for help, there was very little I could say in Arabic to communicate my situation, even though the words *liar* and *cell phone* had been newly added to my vocabulary during the previous night's interrogation and beatings.

I pulled the mask back down over my head and tried to get comfortable enough to sleep. All my life I have slept on my stomach, but now I had to adjust to sleeping on my side or back. Still, with my hands curled in front of me, it was a great relief to finally lie on my back, and I quickly fell asleep.

I awoke several hours later when the door to our room suddenly opened, exposing a shaft of light from the living room into our dark prison. My mask was still pulled down over my face, but I was able to peek through it fairly well by now.

It was Omar, but this time he and his gang members had come for Robert. The men jerked Robert up under his arms and pushed him out of the room. I listened to hear what they would question him about. Robert spoke his native language of Tagalog (one of the major languages used in the Philippines), but he also spoke English fairly well, and my guess was they would question him in English.

Instead, they immediately started beating him ferociously. His screams pierced the air, and then his cries got farther and farther away. I heard a door open, then it slammed shut and the house became eerily quiet.

Where had they taken Robert? I was afraid he was being led away for an execution. We were being held close to a mosque, and all day long the local imam had interrupted my naps as he shouted the calls to prayer. I wasn't sure what time it was, because he had not announced the evening prayers at 8:00, but within a matter of minutes, I heard the imam jabbering in Arabic.

He was talking about a Filipino.

I immediately recognized Robert's voice over the mosque's loudspeaker next; he was crying as he screamed over and over, "*Allah Akbar, Allah Akbar!*" Then I heard the imam announcing the call to prayer with the sounds of Robert screaming and crying behind him.

That's where the guards had taken him—to the mosque. Robert was a Catholic, so I was pretty sure the thugs had beaten him severely in order for him to say that their god was great in Arabic. These were very conservative Muslims, who thought it was their duty to convert everyone they met to their religion, even if it meant beating him into conversion. I guess they thought they could force Robert to convert.

Over the weeks and months of my captivity, the guards would beat me when their leader, Omar, was not around to hear it. They would tell me that if I converted, they would release me. But I never believed them; I'd learned that only Omar had that kind of power. Besides, I was raised Southern Baptist and was not about to convert to Islam.

About an hour after I heard Robert on the loudspeaker, the door opened into the room where I was held, and the guards pushed Robert inside and threw him onto the floor. I was sure they would take me next for more beatings, but they were done for the night.

Robert had not spoken a word to me since we were taken captive, but I wanted to make sure he was not injured from the beatings.

"Are you okay?" I whispered.

There was a long silence. "Yes," he finally whispered back.

Soon after, I heard the sounds of constant machine gun and artillery firing all through the night; the Second Battle of Fallujah was about to begin.

I whispered the Lord's Prayer—and then asked God to get me out of there.

10

MEANWHILE, BACK AT THE MOSQUE . . .

The next day, the guards came into our room after performing their morning prayers and led me outside to go to the bathroom. This would become a routine throughout my captivity. Once in the morning, before sunup, and a second time just after sundown, the guards would lead us outside one at a time to a small area behind a shed to do our business. No toilet paper was available, but we were provided a plastic pitcher of water to wash the mess off our hands. As mentioned earlier, this is common in the Middle East. Yes, it was disgusting. But I became accustomed to it.

Robert and I stayed in the room in complete silence all morning long. It was Friday, November 5, and sometime after noon the guards brought in some white rice, tea, water, soft cheese, and a piece of fruit. After they left, I pushed up my mask to eat and drink. Just minutes later, however, I heard one of the guards coming back to the room, so I quickly pushed my mask back into place.

The door opened, and one of the guards came over to me. At first he just stood there, not saying anything, but finally, he asked me if I knew who had won the presidential election in the States.

I said no, I had not been given any information. Through gritted teeth he said that George W. Bush had won again. Then he hit me in the head with his pistol.

I guess he was a Kerry supporter.

Afterward, I could hear the guards laughing and talking outside, and it sounded like they were kicking cans around the yard. Then I heard a rain of gunfire, the unmistakable sounds of AK-47s. And then more laughing. It finally dawned on me that the guards were throwing the cans into the air and shooting at them for target practice. The racket was shocking, and it was obvious that these guys had no common sense at all. Here we were, in a war zone, and they were outside, shooting guns. It apparently never occurred to them how the Marines might react to the racket. Sure enough, a few minutes later I heard the sounds of mortar fire just above my head; it landed very near. I could hear the men running and shouting in Arabic as they scurried back into the house. So much for target practice.

About an hour after dinner the door to our room opened, and four members of the gang came inside. I was not sure what was going on, but I did not think anything good was going to come of it. The gang members pulled us to our feet and then retied our hands behind our backs. They walked us out of the house and threw us into the trunk of a Toyota Camry and drove around for about five minutes.

When we came to a stop, I could hear a metal gate open and felt the car turn around and then back up inside another compound. I could tell we were near another mosque because I could hear a different imam leading the prayers over the speakers, and it was very loud. I could also hear the sounds of battle on the streets, so I figured we were still in Fallujah.

Not a good sign. Being back at a mosque could mean that they planned to kill Robert and me that very night.

They pulled us out of the trunk and marched us inside what turned out to be a house instead, past a living room and then outside to the backyard and to an outbuilding. It must have been a storage room, but there was nothing in it. The guards left us there on a dirty cement floor and went inside to get something to eat; we got no food that night. The guards came back about an hour later and took us outside to go to the bathroom, then marched us into a small room inside the house for the night.

They pushed me onto the floor and retied my ankles. As I lay there, I prayed to God and asked Him if I was going to make it out alive. It rarely rains in Iraq, so I asked the Lord to give me a sign I would survive, to let it rain just a little bit, so I would know if someone up there, and out there, was thinking about me.

A few minutes later it started raining very softly on the roof of the house. I took it as a sign I would somehow survive. I held on to that hope during my entire captivity.

••••

The next day was Saturday, November 6. The guards retied our hands in front of us—and now they decided to tie our ankles together too. But I didn't complain. At least they had resumed feeding us.

Meals were normally white rice, soft cheese, and a piece of fruit every other day, although most of the time the fruit was near rotting, rarely fresh. Sometimes they even offered us a piece of prepackaged cake. They gave us water and tea three times a day. I was never a big coffee drinker, so I did not miss it. But there were many, many times when I could have used a shot of Jack Daniels whiskey and a cigar.

Just after dinner I heard a couple of new people come into the house.

"We want to play with the American," one of the men said in English.

When I heard that, I was sure they were going to drag me into the living room and beat me. I was really scared, but then I heard the guard tell them no. It seems that Omar was concerned about my high blood pressure. In hindsight, I think that was why they did not drag me to the mosque along with Robert that night for an *Allah Akbar* beating. Maybe my ruse about health would pay off after all.

We were kept at this house (next door to a mosque) for one week, and, finally, we were fed regularly. We also had the luxury of an indoor bathroom that we were allowed to use twice a day. The bathroom was a small attachment to the house; the toilet, however, was just a hole in the floor. Each time, we were given a small pitcher of water to wash our hands when we were finished. Then we were returned to our small room, and our feet were bound together at the ankles. Our hands were tied in front of us so we could eat, and we were still wearing the black ski masks they'd placed over our heads the day we were kidnapped from the Saudi Arabia Company.

Toward the end of the week, on Thursday, November 11, the guards told me negotiations were going well and that I was going to be released soon.

After lunch, they brought me a bowl of water and a cloth to bathe myself, as well as a change of clothes: a dark-tan sweat suit with cuffs in the pants. The days were getting colder and colder, and there was no heat at all in the room where we were being held. Changing clothes made me even colder. Using my toes, I pulled the cuffs down as far around my feet as I could to keep them warm. I hated that they had taken my shoes and socks away that first day. I have always had a thing about wearing socks, even when I sleep.

But I was glad to have the new clothes. I spent the rest of the day lying on the floor, worrying about what kind of pests were in the room with us. I could hear flies buzzing around my head and figured there were spiders, beetles, even scorpions—all common in Iraq—crawling around the room.

I was relieved when the guards came in and told me that a car would be coming for me the next day after sunset to take me back to Baghdad, where I would be traded for money; then I could go home to my family in Memphis.

What a relief. I really had been kidnapped for money and not for some jihadist cause. I wondered how much my ransom had really cost, and who had paid it. The United States did not pay ransoms for citizens kidnapped by terrorists, so I assumed my employer had paid it for me. I was willing to bet the company would want me to pay it back. Maybe I could work it off back in Saudi Arabia. If I ever got out of Iraq, I would not be in any hurry to return. For the first time in nearly two weeks, I was hopeful that I would be released.

And I was eager to see my family. Maybe they didn't even know I had been taken hostage. Perhaps I could just slip back into Saudi Arabia, call the family from there, and pretend that none of this had even happened. I would have to explain to them, or give some excuse, as to why Daddy wasn't sending home as much money as he used to. That was assuming my employer would be deducting a hefty portion to repay my ransom.

I started thinking about how the exchange would actually take place. I was hoping Zein and Mike would be there when I was released, to make sure I was treated well on my return. I was also hoping they'd bring a beer in the car that picked me up. Since Zein was from Amman, Jordan, I thought he would probably fly with me from Baghdad to Amman and then help me get on a plane back to the United States.

On Friday, November 12, I was anxious all day, awaiting the car that would drive me back to Baghdad from wherever I was being held hostage. It was after my dinner of cheese and a piece of rotting banana that I heard the sound of a car pulling up close to the house. Some new men gathered in the living room and conversed in Arabic for about a half hour. Then I heard the men leave and the vehicle's engine start. My heart sank. My ransom had obviously not been paid. But the car was actually moving closer to the house, I realized; I could hear the guard's footsteps coming toward our room. I made sure my mask was pulled around just enough so

I could peek out a little, and I saw the guards walking over to Robert. They were untying his hands and retying them behind his back. Then they walked over to me and did the same thing. This was a signal that we were both about to be moved. Maybe our ransoms had been paid after all.

The men picked me up by my arms and legs, carried me out to the waiting car, and threw me in the trunk next to what smelled like rubber and oil, probably a spare tire. A few minutes later they threw Robert in on top of me.

I was lying on some sort of tire tool, and with Robert's weight pressing me down, the tool was cutting into my back. My head was right next to a rear speaker, and my captors were playing a religious tape very loudly. It was obnoxious. The imam was screaming and even crying. I could tell the recording had been made in a mosque because I could hear the congregation also crying and saying, "*Allah Akbar!*" I had no idea what they were saying on the tape, but they were clearly angry about something. The noise hurt my ears.

The situation made me think of Senator John McCain from Arizona. He had been held as a prisoner of war for six years in Vietnam; a guest, if you will, at the "Hanoi Hilton." He was beaten and tortured regularly. Decades later, after attending a Chinese opera, Mr. McCain compared the event with being tortured in Vietnam. Only he said the opera was worse. Listening to the blaring religious tape, I decided that attending these kinds of religious services would be equally torturous.

The guard drove for about forty-five minutes before stopping the car. I didn't hear any city noise, so I was fairly sure we were not back in Baghdad. The guards got out of the car and started talking to some men whose voices I did not recognize. After a ten-minute discussion, the trunk was opened, and the men lifted us out and carried us around a main house, I presumed, and into an outdoor shack.

They had lied to me for their own entertainment. I guess I really didn't believe the guards were going to let me go, but the new clothes and the fact that they'd let me wash up had given me hope. But they were not setting me free. Just as the September 11 terrorists told the doomed passengers that the planes were merely being hijacked, to keep their victims docile, my kidnappers told me I was being released so that I would not try to fight them or escape during the move to another safe house—the fifth and the creepiest in less than two weeks of my captivity.

11

THE CRITTER SHACK
AND FIELDS OF ROCK

It was November 13, a Saturday, and we were being held in an outdoor shed behind a small farmhouse somewhere in Iraq. I could not hear any city sounds, no traffic, so I assumed we were in the country. We were held captive there for one week.

At the first opportunity, when I thought there were no guards around, I pulled up my mask to survey our new surroundings. I saw Robert lying on his back on the other side of the shack. We did not say a word to each other the entire time we were there.

A long chain looped through the frame of the shed and the metal door, and it was locked with a padlock. It offered us no chance of escape. Worse, the metal door, a kind very common in Iraq, did not extend fully to the floor, and there was at least a two-inch gap that would allow mice and rats to come in and out of the shack.

The walls were made of mud and brick. The roof, if you could call it that, was constructed out of tree limbs and palm leaves, exposing us to the elements and bird droppings.

Guards were posted regularly just outside the shed door. For their entertainment, and to my great annoyance, the guards played cassette tapes of Muslim religious services on a boom box. Loud, screaming, obnoxious imams hollered at their congregations, and the men yelled back in response. Our captors played the tapes night and day.

I remembered back to the night Ramadan had begun just a few weeks before we were kidnapped. Zein and I were on the roof of our house, having cocktails and watching the sun set. All over Baghdad, imams could be heard screaming their calls to prayer over loudspeakers that were attached to minarets at more than a dozen nearby mosques. It was like the battle of the bands—all of the leaders were competing to see who could be the loudest and, in my mind, the most obnoxious. That night the speakers were all cranked up to full volume, and the imams were screeching their heads off.

Zein, who is a Jordanian Muslim, speaks perfect English as well as Arabic. I finally asked him what in the world the imams were yelling about; obviously they were saying more than just "It's time to pray."

"You don't want to know," Zein said with a smile.

"Yes, I do," I insisted.

"They are saying, 'Kill all of the Americans,'" he answered.

In hindsight, he was right: I did not want to know what the imams were saying.

I had lived in the Middle East for more than a decade, and probably 99 percent of the Muslim people I worked with or came into contact with were really fine folks whom I was honored to call my friends. They were hardworking people, like I was, just trying to make a living, pay the bills, and put food on the table and gasoline in the car. But every group of people has its nuts, and it was these extreme wackos who were causing all of the problems, crimes, and insurgencies in Iraq.

Zein was the complete opposite of the Muslims who were holding us hostage. These guards were the type who would go to evening prayers, and afterward, rather than joining their families for meals, they would stay at the mosque to sip tea, eat dates, and devise plots to kill Americans. And the message on the cassette tape the guards were listening to did not sound any different from what the imams were screaming about the night Ramadan began.

But in spite of the screeching nutcase, I could hear birds chirping as they landed on the leafy roof to peck around for food. At night, I could hear what sounded like bats and rats scurrying about on the branches.

For the first time during my captivity, I was thankful to have the mask over my face. Not only did I keep it on during the night, but I would also pull my head down into my shirt as far as I could, to keep the mice I could hear scurrying about the shack away from my face. When the guards fed us rice, I had to be extra careful to not drop any on the ground, because I quickly learned from the tracks they left in the dirt that it would draw mice in at night to snatch up even a single grain.

I worried about the rats and bats, fearing that the creatures might be carrying rabies, and hoping against hope that I would not get bitten. It would have been an extremely painful death. So I fretted constantly about them and those pesky mice.

After a few days worrying about the mice, I instead became concerned that the creatures that *eat* mice—like snakes—might follow their food into the shed. Lots of poisonous snakes inhabit the deserts of Iraq—such as the cobra, whose fangs can deliver fatal venom in a matter of seconds. In addition to the cobras, I knew that about a half dozen vipers were native to Iraq, including the Persian horned viper, Kurdistan viper, desert horned viper, and the deadly saw-scaled viper. One bite from this serpent and you will bleed to death through every orifice in your body.

My training had taught me that these snakes would leave you alone as long as you left them alone. Don't poke them, step on them, or touch them in any manner, and you're safe. Sound enough advice, unless you are blindfolded, hog-tied, and rolling around on the dirt floor of a hut in the middle of God-knows-where.

For the first time, I didn't want to move around at all, and I certainly did not want the guards to hear me, but the bugs were driving me crazy. When I lay on my side, the sandflies would bite my back, and it itched terribly. With my hands bound in front of me, it was impossible to relieve the itch except to roll over onto my back and try to scratch it along the floor. I would have given just about anything for one of those long, plastic back scratchers to rake across my back. Even with my hands tied, I could have done that.

And then there was the tick on my leg. I'm very nearsighted, but I could just make out the little black bug on my right calf. *Great*, I thought. *Now I have to worry about Lyme disease.* My feet were bound, so I tried rubbing my legs back and forth to flick the tick off me, but that didn't work. I then tried scraping my leg across the dirt floor; that didn't work either. It almost drove me mad. I was determined to get that tick off of me, and I fixated on it for hours. I finally positioned myself so that I could hit my leg with my elbow, and after several jabs I was exhausted. As I sat there, gasping for air, I realized that it was not a tick. It was a large mole that had formed on my leg long before I had been taken hostage. I had forgotten about it.

There was no telling how many bugs were actually biting me. My mind was playing tricks on me, and I sometimes felt as though insects were all over me, biting, stinging, and crawling on my bare feet, hands, neck, and clothes.

It's a miracle I survived that week without any deadly contact with creepy critters, and I was so grateful to hear the familiar sounds and activities of the guards as they prepared to move us on Friday, November 19, to another safe house.

Robert and I had grown accustomed to the routine preparations the guards made before we were relocated. The guards would wait until dark, and after they had said their evening prayers around 8:00 p.m., they would retie our hands from the front of our bodies to behind our backs. They would untie our ankles until we walked to the car, then retie the ropes afterward. We would hear a motor rev, and then the guards would lift us into the trunk, me first; usually they just threw Robert on top of me.

Even though I was blindfolded, I knew on this move that we were in the trunk of a Toyota Camry because I owned the same car back in the States. In this model there was a plastic strip that ran along the lower edge of the trunk, and it would constantly fall off, to my annoyance. This time, as I was being thrown into the trunk, the plastic piece indeed fell off, just like it did on my Camry.

We bounced around in the trunk for at least three hours before we stopped at a house, and I heard the guards get out of the car and knock on the door. From the sounds outside, I could tell we were traveling in a caravan: a truck followed behind us, and there was another car in the lead, presumably to spot checkpoints.

About ten people were talking in Arabic. They carried on for the longest time, which was very unusual and very unsettling, because typically they would just rush us straight into a house. But this time the conversation went on for about twenty minutes. I suspected something was amiss, and my suspicions soon proved correct. When they finally took us out of the trunk, the guards untied our ankles, marched us into a shed, laid us down on a dirt floor, and told us to go to sleep. By this time, it was probably 11:00 p.m., but rather than go to sleep, I peeked out from under my mask to see if this shack was filled with vermin and bugs, like our previous accommodations.

What I saw was very unusual. Rather than a bare room, like every other place where we had stayed, this shed was filled with farm tools and heavy equipment that could be pulled behind a tractor to plow and prepare fields for planting. There was a plow on my left side, and on my right side there was a disc harrow that separated Robert and me. It occurred to me that the people at the new safe house either did not know we were coming or had not had time to prepare for our arrival and clean out the shed.

I tried to get some sleep, and I think I dozed off for maybe an hour, when I heard the sounds of the chains coming off the shed doors. This was unnerving; the guards had never bothered us in the middle of the night before.

"Come, come," one of the guards said as he untied my legs and pushed me outside and back to the car's trunk. A few minutes later Robert was dumped on top of me, and the car sped away. I assumed that whoever owned this house was not completely comfortable with us being there and had sent us away.

We drove for about fifteen minutes, and it sounded like we were on a gravel road. When our car stopped, the guards lifted us out of the trunk and untied our feet. We were still blindfolded and barefoot as they pulled us along what was, it became painfully clear, a gravel road. They pushed us across a muddy ditch and then through a dirt field for about twenty yards, and then suddenly I felt asphalt under my feet. It was like a cement patio in the middle of nowhere.

The guards pushed us down onto the ground and ordered us to go to sleep. So here we were: the cars were parked on the road, the guards were walking around us in the open field, it was December and really cold outside, and we weren't wearing any shoes. They tied our feet back up around the ankles, and now they were telling us to go to sleep.

The men jabbered on and laughed among themselves for about fifteen minutes, but the next thing I knew, one of the guards was kicking me in the back. "Get up!" he ordered as he untied my feet, and I could hear the same thing happening with Robert. The guard who'd kicked me stood me up and began pulling me forward by the ropes tied around my wrists. Another guard was behind me, pushing me forward onto the field. There were no plants in the field (it had been plowed over for the winter), and I stumbled helplessly over huge chunks of mud and rocks.

The guards continued to push and pull me up and down the ruts in the field, barefoot and blindfolded, and I could tell they were doing the same to Robert, who was behind me. I could also hear the other guards all around us, laughing and howling as though we were some slapstick midnight movie. Our tormentors must have run us in wide circles at least three times, and I was practically falling down the entire time. I never knew if my foot was going to land on top of a rut or on the row below. It was like water-skiing in a shallow lake. In the dark. With tropical storm–force winds whipping up huge waves of dirt in unexpected places. It was completely disorienting.

At one turn, a large thorn jabbed into my right foot. I tried to yank my hands away from the guard who was pulling me in circles, and I yelled "Wait, wait," but he didn't slow down. I was forced to hop on my left foot and managed to pull the thorn out of my right foot. It must have been at least an inch long, and I could feel my foot bleeding. But that didn't stop the guards from having their sociopathic fun, and they continued to haul us around for another ten minutes before dragging us back to the concrete slab. They finally let go of me and threw me down, and the first thing that hit was my left knee, ripping the cartilage and chipping the bone. Next I heard the sickening crack of bone meeting concrete as my shoulder slammed to the ground, dislocating it. My ankles were swollen for several weeks.

It must have been 2:00 a.m. by that time, and as the guards retied our ankles, they told us to go to sleep, and they threw a blanket over me.

But sleep was an impossible task. The men were talking the whole time, and circling us, like wolves about to move in on their prey. It was probably 4:00 a.m. when one of the guard's cell phones rang, and after a lengthy conversation, the guards retied our ropes and marched us back to the car. One at a time, we were thrown into the trunk.

All in all, it was a screwed-up night; the guards' plans had not gone as they expected, and when we got to the next safe house, it sounded like they still did not have their act together.

The house we were taken to was probably farther from Fallujah, but I could tell we were still in a village because I could hear the constant traffic along the streets.

We were left inside the trunk while the gang members talked outside.

One went inside the house for a few minutes and then came back out, and he was saying something about *madam*. It seems the woman of the house was inside, and they were having a big discussion about it. Muslim women are not allowed to be around men who are not their husbands or family members, and the guards did not seem sure what they should do about it.

After they yammered on for several minutes, I heard another car start and drive away. I assumed that "madam" was in the car and her husband was driving her away, because the whole time I was held there, I never heard a woman's voice. She had been kicked out of her own house just to accommodate Robert and me. Ironically, I felt bad for her.

The guards pulled us out of the trunk and untied our ankles to walk us inside the house. Once inside, they moved Robert and me into a room in what turned out to be a two-story house. An indoor bathroom was directly across the hall.

They left us for the rest of the morning without food.

Skipping meals was again becoming a pattern. Almost everyone in Iraq is on the take in one way or another, and the guards were no exception. Someone was obviously paying the guards to take care of us and feed us, and I later learned this someone was the sheik Omar. But the guards were probably pocketing about 75 percent of the money and using the rest to buy rice and bread and the rotting fruit we were sometimes fed.

But it was just as well we weren't fed that day, as my digestive system finally rebelled, and I experienced an extreme case of diarrhea—all over myself, all over the floor. It was a real mess. And boy, did that really make the guards angry; I could tell by the way they beat me.

The guards took me into the bathroom and then went back into the room where I had made the mess, and I could hear them scrubbing the floor. Scrubbing and cursing me in Arabic.

Finally, they took me to a shower and let me remove my mask to clean myself. It was the first shower I had had in some twenty days, and although

I was quite ill, I enjoyed the shower immensely. Afterward, the men threw some clothes into the room and told me to get dressed; I assume they threw my soiled clothes away. They ordered me to put my mask back on before they opened the bathroom door, and I complied, but instead of leading me out of the room, they pulled off my mask; they were wearing hoods over their heads so I could not see what they looked like. One of the men was holding a 9mm pistol, and he started yelling in Arabic as he pointed the gun at my forehead; then he put it in my mouth. He continued yelling, but I could not understand what he was shouting about.

He pulled the gun out of my mouth, and I said, "*Mafi Arabi*," which means, "I speak no Arabic."

A second guard finally pulled him away from me, and they marched me into a closet and shut the door. In English, one of the guards told me through the door to knock if I needed to go to the bathroom, and they would take me.

I wasn't certain what exactly made me sick. I had been eating a lot of rotten fruit, and lately, the water we were given tasted like dirt. I wasn't claustrophobic, so being locked in the closet did not bother me too much, and I was actually grateful to not have to worry about controlling my bowel movements because, as I had learned, I was not able to do so.

I was in the closet for about four hours, and I could hear the guards still cleaning up my mess and talking on the telephone. I assumed they were talking with Omar to tell him I was sick.

I knocked on the door several times to go back to the bathroom, and true to their word, a guard would come get me and would lead me blindfolded into the bathroom and shut the door. Each time I would pull up my mask and do my business, then wash my hands as thoroughly as I could, as well as the straps that tied my wrists, to prevent me from getting sick again.

After the guards were finished cleaning the room, they took me back in there and threw me down on the wet floor. I ignored the discomfort, which was not nearly as bad as my still-churning stomach.

It would have been nice if the guards had thrown me a little closer to the door, but instead they dumped me clear across the room and retied my feet. When I needed to go back to the bathroom, and I was going a lot that day, I had to scoot myself across the floor like a hog-tied dolphin to tap on the door with my hands.

I was still sick the next day when the guards took me to the bathroom just before sunup, which was the routine. I assumed that the men who had guarded us the previous day had alerted the new guards as to what had happened, and to our arrangement for me to tap on the door when I needed to go to the bathroom.

But I was wrong.

I started tapping on the door when I needed to go to the bathroom, but the guards did not come. I tapped again, more urgently, and this time, the guards came into the room and beat me severely. After they were through kicking and hitting me, they told me to be quiet and not to move or they would beat me again. It was a major strain the remainder of the day, but I was able to control myself until I was taken to the bathroom after sunset.

12

EXERCISE BIKE

Thursday, November 25, I was missing Thanksgiving with my family, and instead of turkey, cornbread dressing, green beans, sweet potatoes, corn, rolls, and some cake for dessert, I was having rice and water.

Actually, I was missing two Thanksgiving celebrations. I had planned to celebrate Thanksgiving Day in Memphis with my daughter, Amanda, and granddaughter, Sabrina, as well as my sister, Barbara. The next day, I had a plane ticket to fly to Ontario Airport in California for a second celebratory dinner with my daughter, Carrie, and my ex-wife, Susan.

My father's birthday was November 25, but he and my mother had both died several years earlier. I was glad they had been spared the terrible pressure of my kidnapping. I thought that if I were going to be killed, at least I would be with them again.

I was really missing my family, and I worried that my kidnapping was probably spoiling their holiday. I truly hoped that they had gone ahead with their dinners as they had planned. I did not want them to be deprived of a good meal just because I was.

It occurred to me that this might just be the first of many holidays I would miss with my family. I had been held captive for nearly a month, and there were no signs that my ransom was going to be paid or that I was going to be let go anytime soon.

"Hey, Robert," I whispered, "do you know what today is?" I'd been keeping careful track of the date in my head, clued in to it by the consistent timing of the prayer calls.

He didn't answer.

"It's Thanksgiving," I said after a few moments.

Still, Robert did not answer. He had not spoken since the night he was taken to the mosque and forced to praise Allah over the loudspeakers, and then he only spoke because I pestered him to let me know that he was okay after the beatings he had suffered.

"It's Thanksgiving," I repeated, but he still did not respond.

Having lived in the Philippines, I knew Thanksgiving was not a big holiday there, but most Filipinos know what the holiday means for Americans. It certainly isn't a big deal in Iraq. However, I worried that the gang might actually kill me on Thanksgiving and videotape the execution to show on television, maybe to make a big political splash and to send a message to the United States.

Before eating my Thanksgiving dinner of rice and water, I prayed and thanked God for my meal. I also asked God to watch over me that night, to make sure that the guards did not kill me.

The next day was Friday, moving day again after the evening prayers, and into the Toyota Camry trunk we were tumbled. The checkpoint car was in front of us, and a truck followed us as we began moving through what sounded like a battle zone. The sounds of gunfire and artillery soon faded to our rear, and I figured we were heading away from Fallujah and probably back toward Baghdad.

I lost track of time, but the trip took several hours, and when we came to a stop, we were lifted out of the trunk and led into the house and into a bedroom. But this time, to my complete surprise and delight, when the guards pushed me to the floor, I landed on a soft foam pad that was about an inch thick.

The foam was so soft my body just sank right down to the floor. The sleeping pad was a huge improvement over the cold, concrete shed floors and our campout on the cement patio. The nights had been getting colder, and this was the first time I was given a blanket to stay warm. I prayed to God and thanked Him as I drifted off to sleep.

The next morning the owner of the house came into the room and began talking to Robert and me in excellent English.

"You need to exercise," he told me. "You do nothing all day, and if you do not move or get exercise, you will die."

That was certainly the opposite of what guards had been telling me for nearly a month. Usually, I was told several times a day that if I moved or made any noise, I would die with a bullet in my head. Instead, I just told him that I was tied up all day and night and that I was not able to exercise. I didn't bother to tell him about the marathon I had run through the plowed field just a week earlier. My ankle did not hurt as much, but I was still in a lot of pain with shoulder and knee injuries.

"I will bring you a bike, an exercise bike, that you can use to get some exercise so you will not die," the man said.

I was not sure at all what to make of this situation. The treatment I received at the hands of my captors differed tremendously from house to house. And this time it seemed as though I had finally hit the jackpot, as far as being held captive was concerned.

True to his word, the next day he came back into the room with this bike of sorts—it was all pipes, a seat, and the two pedals: it looked like one of those cheap things you would buy off of a television shopping network for about forty dollars.

I rode it for about fifteen minutes; my knee popped several times, and my shoulder hurt as well, but I knew the man was right, I did need some exercise. Robert never got the chance to ride it, though. After I was finished, the guards took it away, and we never saw it again.

I could hear the guards in the next room taking turns riding the bike while listening to one of their religious tapes. The men played it over and over with the volume on high, as if the loudness of it all would convince me to convert to Islam. But to me, it was just noise. Insufferable, earsplitting noise.

At night I could hear the guards playing video games. Ironically, one of the games was a mock invasion of Iraq. The game was led in English, which most of the guards could not speak. It just seemed really surreal to me: they were holding me, an American, hostage, while playing a game as an American, attacking Iraq—their own country.

One morning the guards came for me and took me into another room, and when they pulled my mask off, they were all wearing Iraqi scarves covering their heads and most of their faces. Their steely black eyes were all that was exposed.

On a table in front of me was a stack of photos that had been taken from one of the laptop computers stolen from the Saudi Arabia Trading Company. There was a picture of Robert standing in front of the Blackjack mess hall at Camp Victory, and another shot in front of his house while he was holding an MP-5 machine gun.

Me at entrance to Camp Victory

There were also pictures of the Iraqi guards who worked for the company, one of our purchasing agent, and several more of other Filipino workers. The guards pulled out one picture of a twenty-five-year-old female Iraqi employee named Balkese Aden. The man who spoke English asked me if she was a Christian or a Muslim. Although she was wearing jeans and a T-shirt in the photo, and her head was not covered, I told them she was Muslim.

"She must be a bad woman, because she is not properly covered to be a good Muslim woman," the man said.

Next, I was shown a picture of our purchasing agent, Sarmad, standing inside his house with a woman. The man asked me who the woman was, and I said I supposed it was Sarmad's wife, but I was not sure because I had never met her.

"We took these pictures off your computer, so you must know who the woman is," the man said.

I told them these pictures were not on my computer, so I did not know who the woman was. He insisted that the pictures were taken from my computer, and again I told them those pictures were not on my computer. The man asked me what brand of computer I owned, and I told him it was a Toshiba. The man said he would check with the gang member who was pulling information off of the company computers, and get back with me.

I never heard any more about the computers or the pictures. However, after I was questioned, they pulled Robert into the room and questioned him as well. I assumed they were trying to see if our answers matched.

When the guards came in after sunset to take Robert and me to the bathroom that night, one of the men started hitting me on the head and accused me of trying to peek out from under my mask. After he did this on several occasions, I learned to pull the blanket over my head whenever he entered the room so he could not accuse me of peeking.

Meals were served differently here. I was pushed into a corner and told to face the wall. One of the guards would stand behind me and then hand the food around to me. I was told I could raise my mask a little to see the food while I ate. I was sick of eating rice and spoiled fruit and finally mustered up the courage to ask for some meat to eat. The next day they actually brought me a small piece of chicken.

Emboldened by this, I asked for two more blankets, as it was getting colder at night, and again the guards delivered.

I was really beginning to like this place; it was the best I had been treated since I was kidnapped.

But then one night I could hear some new people coming into the house. They conversed in Arabic for about thirty minutes. Any interruption at night, or night visitors, I had learned, was not a good thing.

Suddenly the door opened, and someone spoke to me: "*Kafi halic, Roy?*" or, "How are you, Roy?"

I recognized the voice; it was Omar, the man I assumed was the sheik of the family and the leader of the gang.

"*Quies,*" I responded. *Very good.*

At this Omar kicked me in the back.

"*Mafi quies!*" Omar shouted. *You are not good!*

When the guard came into the room later that night to take us to the bathroom, I pulled the cover up over my head again so he would not accuse me of peeking out from under my mask, but he beat me anyway.

On December 12, the guards told me that a deal had been struck and that I was going to be released. They gave me a large bowl of water and a little bar of soap to clean myself, and a small, torn cloth with which to dry off. They then gave me a new sweat suit to wear that looked just like the other clothes I had been given.

The guards told me that a car would be coming for me the next day; I would be taken to a release point, and then I could fly back to Tennessee to be with my family. They didn't say anything about my ransom having been paid. I didn't really believe them anyway, because had my ransom truly been paid, this news most certainly would have come from Omar.

The next night after dinner, however, a car did come to the house, and the guards began their ritual to move Robert and me. They secured the ropes around our wrists, untied our ankles so we could walk to the car, and then retied them before tossing us into the trunk: me first, and then Robert on top of me.

"Have a good flight back to the U.S.," one of the guards said. "When you see your daughters tomorrow, tell them they should become Muslims."

I later learned that Robert and I had become a package deal: we were being ransomed together, and the kidnappers were now asking for twelve million dollars for both of us. Our worth was declining considerably.

After a forty-five-minute drive the car came to a stop. The trunk opened, and the guards lifted us out, untied our ankles, and walked us barefoot and blindfolded into what seemed like a small storage building.

It was clear to me that this had just been another transfer to a safe house and that neither one of us was going to be released. I was disappointed, but it was a good lesson that I could not believe or trust anything the gang members said to me.

Inside the building I could hear the voices of three men.

"Welcome, welcome," said one of the men, who sounded quite old. "Would you like something to eat?" I later learned his name was Ali Hamid.

"Yes," I said. I had eaten very little that day and very much wanted something to eat.

I felt someone tug at my chin, and one small piece of a tangerine was placed in my mouth; that was it for food. Then the men led me forward. I only took a few steps before I was told to stop. I heard a noise, and then it sounded like someone had jumped down below me, as opposed to climbing up stairs, which I was accustomed to hearing. One of the guards lifted me underneath my arms and then lowered me down into a hole in the floor, an underground cellar. I was thinking, *Do not drop me.* I knew if I broke an arm or leg, no one would look after me.

The last place I was kept hostage, a farmhouse, was in a town called

Al-Mahmoudiyah, about fifteen miles southwest of Baghdad. After reviewing the videotapes of my rescue by Army Special Forces, I could see that it was a large, L-shaped house surrounded by a concrete wall. A family lived in the long section. The guards lived in the shack above our underground cell.

Aerial shot of the house where I was held for most of my imprisonment—underground.

My final prison was a concrete hole in the ground underneath the floor of the smaller section of the house. I was not sure why the family who lived there had constructed the little concrete cellar; it stretched about nine by eleven feet with a ceiling of about four feet—not enough room for anyone to stand. But with the addition and release of eleven other kidnap victims over the next seven months, it appeared the underground prison had been built for just that reason: to imprison hostages underground where we would never be discovered by routine house searches conducted by coalition troops.

Even beneath my mask I could tell it was pitch-black. There was not a speck of light after the guards replaced the trap door over the floor. With no sunlight, I feared there was not enough oxygen for Robert and me.

I thought for sure we would suffocate to death.

13

UNDERGROUND

Our first morning underground I could see nothing but utter blackness when I peeked underneath my mask, but I could hear a lot of activity above me: the guards were watching *Tom and Jerry* cartoons, and two little kids, a boy and a girl, were running around the main house. Morning prayers had already been said, and pots and pans were clanging as the children's mother prepared their breakfast.

The guards were greatly entertained by the cartoons, which are more about slapstick than dialogue, but what few lines were delivered by the mouse or cat were done in English, then dubbed over in Arabic.

Through the guards' laughter I thought I could hear a dog barking, which was odd. Iraqis hate dogs—they equate the animals with pigs, which they believe are unclean—and they do not keep dogs as pets. Given the chance, most Iraqis would shoot dogs, which do run wild throughout the country, or they would run them over with their cars. Most Iraqis I met thought Americans were crazy for even keeping them in the house.

"Bush! Bush! Bush!" an old man was yelling outside. At first I thought something was happening back in the States, that the kidnappers were angry with President Bush for something he had done, something that would surely get me another beating. But then I heard the sounds of a gate opening, and the barking became louder and louder.

The yard area of the house where we were held underground.

"Bush!" the old man yelled again, and I could hear the clinking sounds of dishes. Bush, it turned out, was the dog's name, and the old man was feeding him. I chuckled to myself in the dark. At least the dog was getting fed, and he was probably getting better table scraps than we would get when the guards finally got around to feeding us.

And I was right.

Hamid was the name of the guard who brought us our meals. That first morning, he brought us a piece of bread, some cheese, and a rotting banana. Except for the cup of hot, sweet tea he gave us, I had a feeling I was eating the dog's leftovers.

About midmorning, there was a lot of activity upstairs. There was an uptick in the chatter between the guards, and it sounded like they were moving furniture. A car pulled up to the house, which usually meant we were being moved to another location. But instead, the gang was planning their video debut, starring me.

At the time it was frightening, but in hindsight the whole scene was out of control, like a slapstick cartoon—only these guys had real guns.

The guards hoisted me out of our prison hole, marched me across the room, and sat me down with my back against the wall. One of the guards said they were going to make a videotape of me pleading for my release; he handed me a piece of paper.

"You must put these words in your heart so you can say it for the video without looking at the paper," the guard said. "You must say these words like they were coming from you." What he meant was that I should memorize the script. "I will come back in twenty minutes and we will practice this and then do the video," he said.

"Okay," I responded.

I was thankful they had not given me new clothes to wear—like an orange jumpsuit. Instead, I was wearing the same jogging suit the guards had given me after my bout with diarrhea. It was pretty tacky—gaudy, even: black jogging pants with a heavy black and gold sweatshirt that looked like something out of the 1970s disco era. The left side of the sweatshirt was black, and it was bright yellow-gold on the right side. The collar was black, and there were black patches on the gold sleeves. This sweat suit and others like it were made in China and sold at local bazaars in plastic bags for about three dollars. It was certainly not something I would have worn willingly.

Before he left the room, the guard—or as I thought of him, the script master—lifted my mask up far enough so that I could see underneath and memorize the words.

I did memorize it, and I remember it to this day:

MY NAME IS ROY HALLUMS. I AM AN AMERICAN. I HAVE BEEN ARRESTED BECAUSE IT HAS BEEN PROVED THAT I HAVE BEEN WORKING WITH AMERICAN FORCES. MY LIFE IS IN DANGER. I HAVE BEEN

TRIED AND FOUND GUILTY OF SUPPORTING THE UNITED STATES MILI-
TARY IN IRAQ. I AM NOT REQUESTING THE HELP OF PRESIDENT
BUSH, BECAUSE HIS UNCONCERN FOR THOSE SENT TO THIS HELLHOLE
IS WELL-KNOWN. I AM REQUESTING THE HELP OF ALL ARAB LEADERS
TO HELP ME OUT OF THIS VERY BAD SITUATION. ESPECIALLY PRESIDENT
QADAFI. HE IS KNOWN TO BE CONCERNED WITH PEOPLE WHO HAVE
BEEN IN MY SITUATION BEFORE. I WOULD BE GRATEFUL FOR THE REST
OF MY LIFE IF I CAN BE SAVED FROM CERTAIN DEATH.

Serious words, indeed, for I was in a serious situation—but instead of being concerned for my life, I was trying not to laugh. When the guard first lifted my mask to see, everything was blurry, I had been in total darkness for quite some time, and it took my eyes a while to focus. Without my prescription glasses, it was even longer before I could make out the words, which were written in giant block letters. But it was the paper on which it was written that got my goat; I had not seen this kind since 1954, when I was in elementary school. It was that one-inch-ruled, gray, first-grade writing paper, so raw that wood splinters seemed to lift off the page.

The text was written in very poor English. I caught myself thinking that maybe I could do my captors a favor and clean up the prose a little. Foolish thoughts; now was not the time to be stupid. Anyone watching—including, I hoped, the FBI—would know this is not how an American speaks, and would understand that these were not my words and that I was making the statement against my will. *That*, I thought, *and the AK-47 weapon pointed at my head during the entire video should do the trick.*

Besides, if I changed even one word, the guards might suspect I was trying to send a message, and that would certainly lead to another beating. And anyway, I found it very entertaining that they thought their own country was a hellhole. Finally, something upon which we could all agree.

The script master came back into the room and said he wanted me to practice saying my lines, but instead I challenged him on some of the content. It was apparent to me that the kidnappers had realized they were not going to get the twelve million dollars in ransom from the American Embassy or from my company. They seemed to be making the video as some sort of fishing expedition to see who might pay for me.

"Mu'ammar al-Qadafi is not going to care anything about me or helping with my release unless he gets some kind of deal with the United States," I said.

"No, no, no," the script master said. "You will say this. He has helped other people before."

I learned later that Qadafi had, in fact, paid the ransom for another Filipino man who had been kidnapped, and these guys knew it.

The script master went over the lines with me about five times and then told me he was going to take my mask off, but that I was not to look around the room or at any of the guards. I was to look straight at the camera.

I could tell with my mask still on that the room was brightly lit, and I expected to be blinded by the light and unable to see anything in the room anyway. I closed my eyes as the mask was pulled off, and when I reopened my eyes, I was a little surprised but greatly amused at the scene before me.

One of the guards was acting as the lighting man, and he was holding a mop over his head, with a bald, 100-watt lightbulb taped to the top of the handle. He and the other guards were wearing black and white scarves over their heads that also covered their faces; all I could see were their eyes. (Sunnis actually wear red and white scarves, but they chose instead to wear the color of their enemies, the Shiites, in order to conceal their identity.) Omar was sitting on the floor directly across from me, holding a small video recorder on his knee. He was wearing a black and white *ghutrah* (scarf) with an *igal* to secure it on his head; a dark sports jacket; a long, white Arabic dress called a *thobe*; white socks; and brown, alligator-pattern loafers. The shoes stuck out, as all of the other guards were wearing sandals that are common in Iraq, even during the dead of winter.

Only very wealthy Iraqis wear leather loafers. Later, when Omar stood up, I could see he was about six feet tall and forty pounds overweight.

One man to my left was holding an AK-47, and another guard to my right held a 9mm pistol. The script master stood next to Omar, and there were several guards mingling in the background, also carrying AK-47s.

"Go!" the script master yelled as he pointed at me to start reading my lines.

I got about halfway through the script when he yelled, "Stop! Stop! Stop! You did not say one of the words we wrote down."

Omar had to reset the camera, which made him pretty angry, and he and the script master got into a yelling match about my performance. Under orders from Omar, the guard holding the AK-47 leaned over and started mussing up my hair with his hand. Then he untied my hands.

"When you are talking, rub your hands together like you are very nervous and upset," the script master said. He then ordered everyone back into place, and we started filming again.

I started wringing my hands in an exaggerated fashion. It looked ridiculous, but I started saying my lines again. But just a few seconds into the second take, the script master stopped me again. It seemed that I was still not coming across as desperate enough. I was told that it sounded like I was reading a newspaper.

"We want lots of crying, and to help you cry, we're going to beat you," the script master said.

And they did.

"Take three!" the script master yelled afterward.

I began wringing my hands and saying my lines, but again the script master yelled for me to stop. At this, Omar had had enough, and he started yelling at the script master.

And here is where things got interesting. Omar and the script master were yelling at each other like a couple of prima donnas, as though they were really big-time Hollywood filmmakers defending their turf.

They were completely oblivious to what would happen next with the guards and me.

I felt like I was in the *Twilight Zone*, and that the men were planning to kill me as part of the episode, until the guards let me in on a little secret: they had no ammunition in the guns they were holding to my head. The guard with the AK-47 first leaned in to me and pulled the bolt back on his weapon. "Is okay," he whispered as he exposed the empty chamber to me.

The guard on my right followed suit and pulled the slide back on his 9mm pistol to show me his empty magazine. "Okay." He nodded to me.

Omar and his script master were still squabbling and didn't notice that both of the guards were now sitting Indian-style on both sides of me, our knees touching. The bolt on the AK-47 had jammed, a rare occurrence unless there is a complete and total lack of maintenance of the gun, which was the clear case in this instance.

The guard in charge of lighting noticed what was going on, though, and he put the mop light on the ground and came over to us to help the guard fix the weapon. So there we sat, the four of us, in our little powwow circle with the defunct gun. The guards passed it around and tinkered with it; my hands were untied, but I just kept them in my lap and watched. The lighting guy explained that he had had this problem before with his weapon, and he worked on the bolt until he unjammed it. The guards were congratulating each other on fixing the weapon when Omar finally took notice.

Boy, was he mad.

"I am trying to make a video here!" he screamed in Arabic as he ordered the men back to their positions for another take.

The lighting guy ran back over to his mop and hoisted the light back into the air. He was smiling, very proud he had fixed the gun that was now pointed at my head, with no ammunition in the magazine.

We finished the video without further drama, although Omar said he was mad because of my "bad acting," even after they had beaten me with a leather belt.

Robert made his video next, and cried and pleaded as Omar directed. The only difference in our scripts was that Robert said he would be killed in ten days if his ransom was not paid.

Although we produced the videos in December, I found out later they did not air on Al Jazeera until January 23.

I dreaded the thought of my daughters seeing me on video, beaten and with a gun pointed at my head. The fact that the guns weren't loaded mattered little.

14

RULES OF THE HOUSE

Go into your bathroom, shut the door, push a towel underneath it, and then turn out the lights and curl up on the floor. Try it for fifteen minutes. Now imagine that you are also blindfolded, with a wool ski mask pulled over your head, tied up by your ankles and wrists, and the floor is concrete. For 311 days.

Our underground prison was pitch-black, with or without the ski mask, but I would pull my mask up whenever the guards were not around in order to breathe easier.

I'm not claustrophobic, but I could learn to be. Without a speck of light anywhere, and knowing we were in a concrete hole underneath the floor, I was worried we would run out of air. My breathing often became shallow. Sometimes I gasped for air. Suffocation seemed certain.

And the weather was getting colder. The temperatures were dropping into the thirties at night, but in our cellar the temperatures would hover in the forties and fifties. The moisture from our own breath made it chilly all the time, but at least our captors had given us a blanket and a thin mat to use as a bed.

The day after the gang videotaped my pleas for release, some of the guards came down into our hole in the ground and I could hear them banging something against the wall. They were making all kinds of noise, and I had no idea what they were doing. It turned out they were trying to provide some ventilation and light for the cellar, an effort that would take about three days.

The men had dug a hole through the wall and pushed a white PVC pipe through it until it reached above ground; the pipe would keep the dirt from caving in on the air hole. The guards also ran an electrical wire from upstairs to put in a small light fixture with a 5-watt bulb, just about enough light for a refrigerator.

The underground room.

Because of the war, homes throughout Iraq were experiencing more and more electrical blackouts. The gang used some of the money Omar was paying them to hold us hostage to purchase a generator, and they ran it nearly all day and sometimes into the night. The guards needed the generator to light our little bulb whenever they came down into the cellar to feed us and take us outside to the bathroom. Our host family was also taking advantage of the generator, and from the sound it made, they must have had the whole house blazing with electricity whenever there was a blackout.

I always pulled my mask off as soon as the guards left; it was so dark I could barely see my hand in front of my face. Robert was only a few feet away from me; I could have touched him if I'd inched closer. The little light coming on signaled to me that the guards were getting ready to come into our hole, and it also gave me brief opportunities several times a day to survey my new permanent surroundings.

Robert, however, never lifted his mask; he wore it the whole time he was in captivity. After his release in June, he wore sunglasses day and night because of the damage the darkness ultimately did to his eyesight. I later asked my doctor whether rebelling against the kidnappers and removing my mask every chance I got had perhaps saved my eyesight, but he said he doubted it had made any difference. (Months after I was rescued, I had LASIK surgery performed and no longer require glasses. My eyesight today is better than it was my entire life before the surgery.)

When we were taken outside for our morning bathroom break, it was usually just after sunrise, and I could see some sunlight underneath my mask. For our nightly bathroom breaks, it was already dark outside. We were obviously out in the country, as there were no lights from any nearby city. It was a challenge to take care of business in the black of night.

Our "bathroom" during our underground captivity.

Back in our underground hole, there was nothing to do but to wait, and listen. I always believed I would be rescued; I was certain that the Army and my government were doing everything they could to find me. I was ever hopeful. But the days in December went by slowly. Because I could not see or do anything, I listened to every little sound to figure out what was going on in the guardhouse directly above me and the main house attached to it.

I could hear people walking around; sometimes I could hear the old man yelling for his dog. "Bush, Bush, Bush!" There was a cow nearby, and whenever I heard it moo, I wished for a cold glass of milk. Or a steak. Or a hamburger. With fries.

Whenever I heard the metal gate open and close, I would wonder who was coming or leaving the house. I could hear the little boy (who was about six years old, I'd guessed) running and playing, and his four-year-old sister toddling after him. There was also a small baby I could hear crying.

It was unbelievable to me that these people would put their children in the middle of such a dangerous operation, but in Iraq this had become common. Whenever there was some kind of military action and the media would report that women and children were killed, it was because the men deliberately put their families in harm's way. You could tell a guilty man by how many women and children he surrounded himself with—they were always right there in the middle of everything. An uncle would be in the living room, shooting at U.S. troops, and the women and children would be in the kitchen, making lunch, and would end up getting killed when their house was blown up.

I was thinking a lot about my family this month, what with Christmas and New Year's Eve approaching. I lay there in the dark, tied up, wondering what was going on back home in Memphis with Amanda and my sister, Barbara, and with Carrie and Susan in California. I knew this would not be a very good Christmas for them. I had missed holidays with them before when I was in the Navy, but those were obviously different situations, because they always knew I was safe, even if they did not always know where I was stationed or deployed.

I was also missing Carrie's birthday on December 19—and our yearly shopping expedition. As her birthday fell so close to Christmas, I never wanted her to miss out on having her own birthday celebration, so I would take her shopping to buy whatever she wanted—a new outfit, shoes, handbag, or electronic gizmo. Taking her shopping for her own birthday present also ensured that she always got exactly what she wanted. I had planned my Thanksgiving break in the States to be with Carrie on her birthday. Now I thought of the dinner I would have taken her to, the cake I would have ordered for her. I knew I was ruining her birthday.

Carrie always planned her party months in advance, so her friends and the family would remember to pencil the event in on their calendars along with other holiday parties. But this year she canceled it. "It would have felt weird to have had a party," Carrie later said. "Parties are for celebrations, and I had nothing to celebrate."

Instead, Carrie and Susan made their first network news appearance on *Good Morning America* on December 19, to take my name and the story of my kidnapping public for the first time.

Susan was fed up with keeping my kidnapping a secret, and when she first saw my name pop up on an Internet blog called The Jawa Report, she told the FBI she wanted to go public. The FBI did not want media attention during the first few months of the ordeal because they were afraid it might interfere with any negotiations with the kidnappers. But her FBI handler decided it would give Susan some comfort (or even stop her from going to the media) to meet with members of another family whose loved one had been held hostage.

An Al-Qaeda–linked group had kidnapped Martin and Gracia Burnham in 2001 while the couple were celebrating their eighteenth wedding anniversary on Palawan Island in the southern Philippines. The two missionaries were held captive for more than a year before Filipino soldiers found them and launched a rescue attempt. Tragically, Martin

Burnham was killed and his wife was injured during the two-hour fire-fight for their release. Their ordeal was all over the media during the time it occurred. However, the FBI arranged a meeting with Alberto Sobero, whose brother Guillermo had been kidnapped at the same time as the Burnhams. Guillermo was held hostage with the Burnhams for only two weeks before the terrorists decapitated him. (The terrorists told the media afterward that Guillermo's death was a gift to their country on Independence Day.)

"The FBI told me that Alberto would know more about how I was feeling and that we could relate to each other," Susan said. "He told me his family had disagreed on how to handle the situation and whether they should involve the media. Our family had mixed opinions as well. The FBI told us to stay quiet, not to tell anyone Roy had been kidnapped, not even our friends. But Alberto said they had used the media as a tool to communicate to the kidnappers. And that was the first time it ever occurred to me to use the media to our advantage."

Susan continued. "I told Carrie about our meeting, about using the media as a tool. It had been more than a month since Roy was taken, and now the FBI was telling us he was sick," she said. "I was afraid that Roy might think we didn't even know he was kidnapped, or that we didn't care. So I picked up the phone and I called the Associated Press."

It was common for kidnap groups to tell whomever they were nego-tiating with that their hostages were sick or in poor health, but it was just a ploy to speed up negotiations and get their money quicker. The kidnappers also thought that lying about the health of their captives would give them an upper hand with the family.

I believe that my kidnappers, who were negotiating our release with the owners at the Saudi Arabia Trading Company, must have told them I had high blood pressure. I regret that my little white lie caused my family concern, but in the end I think it saved me from more severe beatings. And now, the word was out that it was the American Roy Hallums who had been kidnapped and was being held hostage by Iraqi militants.

"The media came to my house, and they were lined up and down the street," Susan said. "Someone knocked on the door, and I opened it, expecting a local reporter, but it was a lady who said she was with *Good Morning America* and asked if we could leave for New York in two hours. So I called Carrie and told her to pack her bags. Carrie thinks Roy is the world's greatest dad; she adores him—and since it was her birthday, I was hoping she could have some good moments in New York."

"I felt guilty the whole time I was there," Carrie later said. "I had always wanted to go to New York, but the trip was bittersweet. I looked at it as a business trip; we were trying to do a job and get my dad's name out to get him released. It was very hard to do the interview, though, because I was talking about something that was very painful."

The network sent a car to take Susan and Carrie to the airport while a caravan of media followed. "The reporters even followed us onto the plane. I've never seen anything like that in my life," Susan said.

Their plane landed in the middle of the night in New York, and another throng of reporters was there to greet them. "The network didn't want us to talk to any other media, so they met us at the airport and packed us into another car and led us on a wild ride through the city," Susan said. "It was snowing, and it felt like we were driving a hundred miles an hour."

The car pulled up to the Essex House on Central Park, but it was a ruse. Rather than checking in, Susan and Carrie fled through the lobby and out another door, where a car was waiting to pick them back up to take them to a boutique hotel in Times Square, called the Muse. To further protect their scoop, ABC registered them under false names.

"Carrie had been through a rough time, and it was good for her to see the beauty of New York and to see the skyline," Susan said. "She just had so much weight on her shoulders, and it was her birthday. But I knew she felt like she was in the middle of a bad dream the whole time we were there."

Susan also appeared on CNN on December 18 and told the

interviewer that the government was not sharing any information about my situation—"zero information" is what she said.[1] The lack of information made it harder on my family to cope with my situation.

"But the main thing that the family wanted to say was . . . pray for his safety and his return and that he's being treated well and humanely and to please let him come home," Susan said. "This is the holidays. Everyone's supposed to be happy now. And we're devastated."[2]

On December 21, a story in the *Press Enterprise* in Riverside, California, said that Susan "believe[d] drawing attention to her ex-husband's plight might help. For weeks, Susan Hallums kept her secret," the paper reported. "She did not explain to neighbors and friends the personal significance of an American flag in front of her home or the sign in the window that said 'Free our American hostage in Iraq.'

"'We weren't supposed to tell anybody,' Susan told the reporter. "But after reading coverage about one of the other captives," the article continued, "and finding her ex-husband's name in a report on a Web site, Susan Hallums decided to speak out about the man she calls quiet, patient and well-liked. She hopes bringing attention to his plight will do some good."

"We felt like we couldn't share anything," Susan said in the interview. "It's been six weeks now. It's terribly hard to talk about it, but it feels better to talk than to have to not disclose something. It's a release."[3]

As Christmas approached, I wondered if the Sunni Muslims would use the occasion to send a message to America by killing me—would they kill me on Christmas Day or beforehand and videotape my murder to be shown on Al Jazeera television?

My fears were reinforced when one of the guards instructed Robert and me on the "house rules." I learned about these rules one mid-December morning after we were taken outside for our routine morning bathroom break. Rather than being returned to our hole in the ground, Robert and I were taken into the main house and forced to the floor on our knees.

One of the guards poked me in the head with his finger and said, "You read this." He handed me a piece of paper and pulled my mask up over my nose so I could look down and read it. The paper had been seemingly torn from a first grader's notebook, and the rules were written in large block letters. It read:

ONE — WE ARE YOUR FRIENDS, WE ARE GOING TO HELP YOU.

TWO — WE ARE GOING TO BRING FOOD AND MEDICINE.
      JUST ASK FOR IT.

THREE — IF YOU NEED ANYTHING, JUST ASK FOR IT.

FOUR — IF YOU TALK TO ANYONE, WE WILL KILL YOU.

FIVE — IF YOU DO BAD ACTING, WE WILL KILL YOU IMMEDIATELY.

That really cracked me up, silently. *They are my friends, but they will not hesitate to kill me.*

The guard poked me in the head again. "Do you understand?"

I nodded that I did, and he moved on to Robert and had him read the house rules as well. Once Robert assured the guard he understood the rules as well, we were put back down into our hole.

As the days progressed, our day-to-day lives became a routine.

We were usually served three meals a day. For breakfast, the guards would bring us cheese and pita bread. The soft cheese came in a package with a smiling cow on the label with the Swiss Alps in the background. The label read *Happy Cow Cheese.*

For lunch they would serve us rice and a soup broth, along with hot tea. Dinner was more of the same. Sometimes they would put a piece of chicken in the broth or another piece of meat; other times we would get what looked like a child-size chicken finger. Rather than being fried, it was boiled. Occasionally the guards would treat us to a piece of fruit or a vegetable, but it was usually rotting and would probably have been thrown away if not for us hostages. It was as if we were human compost piles hidden underneath the house.

The entrance to the underground cell.

Months later, when the guards began cementing over the door and abandoning me underground for three days at a time, they would bring me nine cans of sardines; some rotten fruit, like apples and bananas; and water in a two-liter container that once contained Coke or Diet Coke. But there was one time when they brought me water in a green bottle with Arabic writing on the label, and it had a lemon-lime flavor. As the guards were climbing up the ladder and out of the hole, I peeked underneath my mask to check out the bottle. (Once they were out, it would be lights out for three or four days until I would be dug out and fed again.) I turned the bottle around to see if there was an English translation of the soda brand.

The label read *Cheer Up!*

I smiled, but it did not exactly cheer me up.

15

JANUARY

Company was coming.

After being held hostage in an underground cellar with Robert for more than a month, it was January—and the guards told us they had captured more hostages, who would soon join us in our dark prison. As they gave us our morning bread and Happy Cow Cheese, they warned us that we must not speak to or look at our new guests. (As if we could even see what they looked like in that pitch-black hole.)

They reinforced their warnings by giving Robert and me a good beating apiece—an action that was not included in the house rules, but as I now knew, Iraqi rules were always subject to change on a whim. Although the rules said they were our friends and would take care of us and feed us, it said nothing about intermittent beatings. Often when the guards would take us outside to go to the bathroom, they would hit us in the back or the stomach before they pushed us back into our hole. It didn't happen every day, but I never knew when to expect a beating, and it never seemed to correspond to anything Robert or I had done.

In an effort to disguise our identities from the newly arriving hostages, the guards gave us new nicknames; Robert was to be called Faddie, and my new name was Shaddie.

Before the guards brought the new captives into our hole on January 13, our physical discomfort got even worse. We were already hog-tied and blindfolded; now the guards raised our masks just enough so they could stuff toilet paper in our ears and then lowered our masks and wrapped tan masking tape around our mouths.

The guards had used this trick with the masking tape several times while they were moving Robert and me from safe house to safe house. But they'd stopped doing it after one incident in which they nearly killed me after wrapping the tape so tight around my nose and mouth that I could not breathe. I shook my head violently until they removed the tape over my nose.

This time the guards took a little more care to just wrap my mouth so that I could not speak to the new hostages, and the toilet paper stuffed in my ears, they thought, would prevent me from hearing much of anything.

Ironically, as the guards were climbing the stairs out of our little hole, one of them stopped and said, "Remember, no talking, no looking."

The steps leading down into the underground prison cell.

Both Robert and I responded, "Yes, yes."

The fact that we had heard him and were able to speak to answer him escaped him completely.

"Good," he said, and closed the trapdoor above us.

Around noontime I could sense movement in the room above me, and then two new prisoners were brought down into the cellar. I later learned it was French journalist Florence Aubenas, who worked for the Paris daily newspaper *Libération*, and her Iraqi translator, Hussein Hanoun al-Saadi.

For the first two weeks we were unable to communicate at all. When the guards would bring us food, they had to remove the tape from our mouths, then replaced it after we were finished eating. They did this three times a day.

Sometimes the guards would wrap the tape below the edge of the mask and over the lower part of my ear and onto my cheek, which proved to be quite painful when they ripped it off for each meal. The tape would also pull some skin off my face, and the guards would just put the tape back over the wound, only to yank it off six hours later.

On the fourth day of this ritual, I finally asked one of the guards how long they planned on doing this.

"Not long, not long. We have to do this because it is very important," he said.

That was all I needed to know. In the Middle East, something might be super important when they think of it, but if they have to do something for themselves over a number of days or it otherwise involves work, the task will quickly become not that important at all, and they will stop doing it. That's why nothing ever gets done in Iraq, and why their government can never accomplish anything.

So I knew the guards would not keep this up forever, although they did continue the taping ritual longer than I thought they would. It was eight days later when suddenly taping us up and stuffing toilet paper in our ears was no longer "very important." I didn't get an infection, but I had sores on my face that took at least a week to heal.

Even with the tape removed, it was at least a month before I spoke to Florence.

Hussein was another matter. He was a Shiite Muslim, and while our Sunni guards often beat him because of the animosity between their religions, they still allowed him to pray anytime he wanted to pray in our cellar. The guards even pointed out the direction of Mecca so Hussein could pray in the proper direction.

It was an interesting development. I didn't know where I was at the time, but it was a safe assumption that we were being held in the Anbar province, the violent home of the Sunni insurgency, where the presence of American troops was rare. (I later learned that my assumption about my location was correct.) The province is so large that it stretches from Baghdad in the geographic center of Iraq and borders Saudi Arabia. Muslims in Iraq always face southwest when they pray toward Mecca in Saudi Arabia. And now I knew which way southwest was. It was a gotcha moment.

As Hussein pulled himself onto his knees with his back turned away from the hole in the floor above us, I could feel him shift himself to face the left corner of our little cell, and then he began his prayer bows, his feet overlapping mine at times.

Inside the cell.

Thoughts of escape filled my head. Now I knew the way to Mecca; now I knew which direction to run to reach Saudi Arabia, where I might be safe. I filed this information away in case I ever got the chance to get out of there. I would need a car, though, and then it occurred to me that I would need someone to escape with me to read the road signs to Saudi Arabia, because the guards had destroyed my glasses.

As I dreamed of escape there in the dark, Hussein prayed to be rescued. Hussein, as it turned out, prayed a lot.

Muslims pray in a very low voice, because they only intend for it to be heard by Allah, so even though Hussein was right next to me, I could not make out what he was saying as he bowed and mumbled, bowed and prayed softly, bowed and prayed more, prayer after prayer after prayer. At first I thought prayer was good—we should all be praying. But after three hours of nonstop prayer, I thought, *Give it a rest, buddy*.

And then he did rest. And he snored. Like a freight train.

He prayed all day long, about eighteen hours, and then he would snore through the rest. This went on day after day, week after week, month after month. I had survived beatings, torture, rats, snakes and bugs, sickness, filth, and starvation, but this guy nearly drove me crazy. He was a one-man noise machine.

Hussein was only about three inches away from me, and he would prop his ankles over my feet like an anchor as he prayed toward Mecca. Over and over, I would push him off and whisper to him to scoot over. I didn't mind the fact that he was praying; I just didn't want him doing it on top of me.

And where was he getting all of these prayers? Muslims only have so many prayers that can be recited, but Hussein had enough prayers to fill an entire day. I finally decided he must be reciting whole verses from the Koran, and at the rate he was going, he was going to repeat that holy book from beginning to end. More than once.

16

VIDEO RELEASE

A month after Omar and his film crew recorded the video of me pleading for my life, the tape was released to the media. It was January 24. As I had predicted, it devastated my family to see me having been beaten, begging for help, with a gun pointed at my head.

Carrie had done several television interviews in December, and then the attention had died down. But with the release of the video, there was a renewed interest in my story, and the networks started calling Susan and Carrie again for interviews.

"It was hard enough to do the first interviews in December, because the whole situation was so painful," Carrie said. "It just got worse when I went back to New York to do the *Today* show with Katie Couric. The network producer called me at 4:00 a.m. and told me about the video. But I didn't actually see it until I was on the set, being interviewed live on television—they showed the video directly behind me on a screen. Dad looked terrible, and he was acting odd. He was moving his hands and making gestures like I had never seen before. And the things he said, I could tell he was being forced; I knew those weren't his own words.

"From watching the video of my father," Carrie continued, "I could tell he was being tied up, because there were plastic cuffs around his wrists that had been cut so that he could wring his hands. It looked like there was a black scarf around his neck, which most likely was used as a blindfold. Dad has very poor eyesight and was not wearing his glasses," Carrie said. "I saw bruises on his head, and he was practically gasping for air as he spoke. I was afraid he would not live much longer and that he was ill. I also thought I could hear a baby crying in the background."

Also appearing on the *Today* show that morning was country music singer LeAnn Rimes, who performed "How Do I Live" during the show. Carrie said the song was heartbreaking, and that afterward, LeAnn gave her a big hug.

Ann Curry, who did the actual interview, went out of her way to make Carrie feel comfortable and welcome. Nonetheless, Carrie had had her fill.

"After a while, it just got too hard to do the interviews because they would always replay the video while I was talking," Carrie said. "Watching it over and over and over, I started to have nightmares, because I had such a strong visual image of my dad and what was happening to him. So I stopped doing the shows; I just couldn't handle it anymore."

Amanda had refused to do any media appearances. She said she would only talk to reporters after the kidnappers released me. But that didn't stop the media hordes from intruding on her life and disrespecting her privacy. Reporters would trespass on my property, where Amanda was living with her daughter, Sabrina. They would bang on the doors, peek inside windows, even chase her into the garage. The events left Sabrina in tears.

They weren't even safe at the grocery store, where Sabrina saw my face on the front page of the newspapers. "Having your father kidnapped by terrorists isn't something that many families experience," Amanda said. "And the pain that my child experienced was so enormous, all I could do was try to be strong for her."

It brought no comfort to my children when the FBI contacted Carrie and asked her where my remains should be sent. Carrie asked if they had found my dead body, and they said no, they just needed the information for their records. Carrie called her mother and relayed the conversation. Susan was upset at hearing this and asked the FBI to call her first about this type of information.

Until the video surfaced, the Hostage Working Group assumed I was dead. The kidnappers never approached the American Embassy, because they knew Americans will not negotiate with terrorists.

"United States policy is to make no concessions to terrorists, but we will talk with anyone to bring an American hostage home," Dan O'Shea said later. "If we can resolve the situation by talking, we will talk to the bad guys—but kidnappers in Iraq weren't in the habit of calling the American Embassy. Our goal and our mission were to recover Roy. We wanted to have conversations with them; we wanted to make sure Roy was still alive." He went on, "We got a message that because they could not get negotiations or payment for Roy's life, they were going to sell him to Al-Qaeda and that he was a dead man."

Because I was not wearing an orange jumpsuit and there were no mujahideen holding guns featured in the video, O'Shea concluded that I had not been traded to Al-Qaeda after all. Intelligence analysts at the Hostage Working Group studied every little detail in the video to search for clues as to what group had taken me and where I was being held captive.

"The video was a good sign; it was the first bit of news we had on Roy," O'Shea said. "Within days of his kidnapping, the Second Battle of Fallujah kicked off, and that took the focus off of everything; Zarqawi was running for his life. Because of that and a host of other events, we had no solid information on Roy right away. We looked at the video to first verify it was Roy and then determine how recently it had been shot, what kind of clothes he was wearing, and whether he was being fed or was losing weight." He continued, "They were trying to hide the surroundings where they videotaped him, because it was in a very dark room. It looked like he was being held in a cellar, literally in a hole in the ground."

In early 2005, multiple intelligence reports came in concerning Western hostages being held with other Iraqi captives. After local Iraqi families paid ransoms averaging twenty to thirty thousand dollars—many times the entire family savings—released survivors would recount the horrors. They were held in farmhouse hostage factories, blindfolded and stacked next to other victims in cramped quarters smelling of sweat, blood, and human excrement, treated like animals by their captors.

When ransoms were paid and hostages released, they would tell authorities about other victims with whom they'd been held, but most times they did not know the names of the other victims. If these leads could be translated into general locations, the military would send patrols to follow up on them.

"At one point, a specific call came in regarding Roy Hallums, but it never led to anything conclusive. On more than one occasion, Army Special Forces were dispatched to search for him at different locations, but they did not recover any hostages," O'Shea said.

Bureaucratic red tape would eventually put a stranglehold on O'Shea's investigation and his efforts to find me.

"The FBI's attitude toward kidnapping was, if it wasn't an American who was taken hostage, then they were not interested in dedicating significance," O'Shea continued. "They always had agents assigned to the organization and attended every Hostage Working Group meeting, but their average tours of duty were only ninety days and there was limited continuity." The Hostage Working Group had a tough time putting all of the pieces of the puzzle together because they did not limit their investigations to American cases only. The group handled every kidnapping, hundreds of Iraqi locals and foreign hostages—including some very high-profile foreign correspondents who would later be held hostage with me.

"There was so much raw data and new cases coming in every day, we could only write up our daily report and pass on raw data to the intelligence analysts trying to connect all the dots leading to that elusive action-able intelligence and a ten-digit grid or exact position of Roy Hallum's location," O'Shea explained.

The Hostage Working Group personnel were doing the best job they could, but the bureaucracy was inefficient for what they were doing. The FBI agents assigned to my case could not travel outside the safety of the Green Zone into the so-called Triangle of Death (a geographic area south of Baghdad, formed by Baghdad, Al Hillah, and the Euphrates River)—and that is where I was being held. Another maddening part of the puzzle was that I was the only American-born citizen this particular gang had kidnapped, although they'd abducted more than a dozen Iraqis, French, Filipinos, Romanians, and one Iraqi with American citizenship.

While American Special Forces were focused on looking for Zarqawi, they were also looking for me. They knew I was ex-military; whenever they got a lead on kidnap victims and went out on missions, they were hoping to find me.

On January 25, the guards came into the cellar and pushed us all against one wall and told us not to move. Then they went into a beating frenzy. They started with Hussein, then moved on to Robert and slapped him across the face and whacked him on his backside. A guard, whose name I learned was Hamid, punched my head several times. It almost knocked me out; all I could see was black and stars.

Two more hostages were brought into the cellar—Amar Obati and his son Yasser—and the guards beat them severely. I later learned that Amar and Yasser had fought back when the kidnappers stormed their home in Baghdad, and the guards were taking out their frustrations on all of us. Amar surrendered to the kidnappers after they held a gun to Yasser's head and threatened to shoot him in front of his mother.

After the beatings the guards climbed up out of the cellar and closed the door, leaving us in complete darkness.

17

THE FAMILY TAKES ACTION

Back home in the United States, Carrie created a public Web site on which she posted photos of the family and me, as well as news of my situation and events the family held to bring attention to my kidnapping. The site ultimately drew in more than eighty-five thousand viewers, but Carrie was forced to abandon the whole project after some less-than-sympathetic readers posted nasty notes.

"People would write in and say they could not wait to see the video of my father's head being chopped off. There are a lot of psychotic nuts out there," Carrie said. "Then people started posting the Web addresses of porn sites and offers to sell drugs. I tried e-mailing them back to tell them this was a memorial site, but they just kept posting more smut. It upset my mom, so I finally abandoned the Web site, and it was a huge weight off my shoulders."

Instead, Carrie kept her innermost thoughts in a diary that she shared with me after my release. As I read through Carrie's diary, I discovered that she was pretty much coping with my kidnapping the same way I was. On February 9, she wrote:

Sometimes I don't know if I can make it through this, but somehow, I make it to the next moment, then to the next hour, and finally the next day. People keep talking about how strong I am. I don't feel strong at all. Actually, I feel very weak. I want to save my Dad but I can't. I feel so small. I am starting to have lots of anxiety all the time now. I'm getting panic attacks that last all day. I can't sleep, and when I do I have nightmares. I am jumpy and irritable. I don't feel strong at all. If I were stronger, I wish I could have convinced my dad to not go back to the Middle East when I saw him in June. I don't think I tried hard enough. I didn't want him to feel guilty for going, which is why I didn't push harder for him not to go.

Two days before Valentine's Day, Carrie wrote:

Today I had a good dream about my dad. He had been released and I was hiking with him and my sister. He was okay in my dream. I hated to wake up. I slept as long as I could. I think for at least three or so hours. I'm feeling pretty lonely right now. If I lose my dad, then I know I'll never be loved by anyone as much as I was loved by him. I will miss him so much. Actually I already do. Everything around me reminds me of him and things we have done together. I just hope and pray he is okay and that his kidnappers will release him. I don't know what I will do without my dad. I love you, Dad. Please be okay and come home soon. Love always, your daughter, Carrie.

On Valentine's Day, when she should have been sharing a loving day with her husband, Rob, her thoughts still turned to my abduction. "Hearts and kisses," Carrie wrote. "Went to Disneyland with Rob. Still thought about my Dad all day. I felt sad, even at Disneyland." She drew a frowny face next to the entry.

Amanda rarely called her mom or sister during my ordeal. "I had always been close to my mom and sister, but I was blocking everything out. It was all just too horrible, and I had to be strong for my daughter, for my dad's granddaughter," she said later. "I never believed it was my dad who was taken anyway, because he told me he was working in Saudi Arabia."

Amanda tried to keep up a normal life at home and learned to turn off the news when Sabrina was in the room. Reports of my hostage situation on the local news channels would leave the little girl in tears. Sabrina was also having a hard time at school—even children in the second grade were aware of my kidnapping. "They would talk about her grandfather and ask her if he was going to be killed," Amanda said. "It shut down her life."

Carrie was frustrated that the FBI was not sharing information as to who might have kidnapped me, where I might be being held in Iraq, or any rescue attempts. "I thought they could not tell us anything because it was classified information. I asked them what they were doing, and they said they had someone looking for him. 'Your father is in another country, where there is a lot of red tape; we can't just go in there,' one of the FBI agents told me. My response was, 'But we are occupying this country.' It seemed like the FBI had a lid on every bit of information about my father," Carrie said. "There was hardly any mention of him in the media in the United States; it seemed like there was a complete blackout on information by the FBI." She continued, "I discovered that the newspapers in the Philippines were carrying several stories about Robert, and I was able to pick up some information about who might have taken my dad. That's where I learned about the ransom demands. Interestingly, when I told the FBI about the details I had gleaned from those newspapers in the Philippines, the articles came to a halt. It was as if the agents called across the Pacific Ocean and yelled, 'Stop the presses!' I felt like they spent more time preventing us from getting any information than actually looking for my dad.

"The FBI did tell me that my dad was in really bad health and that the kidnappers had requested some medication," Carrie said. "The FBI said that they had gotten some medication to my dad. I asked them point-blank, if you could get medication to my dad, why can't you rescue my dad?"

Carrie wasn't the only one who was frustrated by the FBI; Susan was, as well, and had reason to believe the agency tapped her telephone.

One of my colleagues at the Saudi Arabia Trading Company, Bandar Antabi, called Susan and told her that negotiations with the kidnappers had broken down. The gang had been negotiating with the company since the first day, trying to collect a large ransom. He suggested she get a passport and go to Doha, Qatar, to try to restart negotiations and secure my release. Susan had researched and found articles in a Lebanese newspaper that reported that Mu'ammar al-Qadafi helped in the release of some Philippine hostages. She decided to call the Libyan Embassy in Washington, and when she reached a senior official there, she asked that a letter she wrote be forwarded to the Libyan leader.

"The FBI had to be listening, because they called me and told me they did not want to see another Hallums get kidnapped and that I could not go to Qatar," Susan said.

Susan also considered going to Tripoli to help secure my release. Flights into Libya from the United States were banned in 1992 after Qadhafi gave refuge to two of his countrymen accused of blowing up a Pan American jetliner in 1988 (270 people were killed). "The FBI agent said, 'What are you going to do, charter a plane into Tripoli? You can't go there,'" Susan reported later. "And I eventually agreed."

The FBI also told Susan that my kidnapping was an inside job, and that Bandar could be involved. But Susan disagreed. "After talking to Bandar several times on the phone, I refused to believe he could have had anything to do with Roy's kidnapping. Bandar was my angel of mercy, and he was giving me much-needed information," she said.

"We started talking on other people's cell phones because we thought we were being monitored, and we would e-mail each other in code. It was mind-boggling at the time—I was living in the greatest country in the world, home of the free and the brave, yet my own government appeared to be spending most of its time spying on me rather than trying to find my husband of thirty years," Susan said.

Susan called New York Senator Hillary Clinton, because she was looking for anyone who might be able to help, but a staffer told her they only handled casework for constituents in her state. Susan told them I was born in Arkansas, but was told the senator was too busy helping people in New York. Next she tried getting help from California Governor Arnold Schwarzenegger, but his office referred her to the State Department in Washington. Then she called California Senator Dianne Feinstein's office.

"She is wonderful; she's a shark," Susan said. "I became friends with Peter Cleveland, her chief of staff, and he always called me and kept me up-to-date on meetings they were having with the FBI and encouraged me to keep doing media interviews. I asked him if what I was doing was wise; the last thing I wanted to do was to bring Roy harm. There were some things Peter could not talk to me about that were classified information, but based on what he was hearing, he said the media attention was helping."

What also helped Susan at the time was reading a book about the kidnapping and escape of a Halliburton truck driver in Iraq by the name of Thomas Hamill. His convoy of trucks was attacked in April 2004, and Hamill and six other drivers were taken hostage. His captors were demanding that American forces withdraw from Fallujah, but the forty-three-year-old from Macon, Mississippi, managed to escape on his own just three weeks after he was kidnapped. Hamill broke out of the house where he was being held after hearing sounds of an American military convoy passing nearby. He took off his white shirt and waved it as he ran toward the convoy, yelling that he was an American prisoner of war. While Hamill escaped with his life, four of the other truck drivers were later found dead south of Tikrit.

During his captivity, Hamill's wife, Kellie, made television appearances and pleaded for his life, and this gave Susan hope she was doing the right thing. Amanda and Susan drove down to meet Tommy Hamill in Mississippi, where they were greeted with hugs and kisses. Susan said it was a wonderful lunch and that Tommy transported them back to Iraq with the story of his ordeal. They all prayed for my safe return that day and hoped for a miracle.

18

AMERICA'S FUNNIEST HOME VIDEOS

I was understandably surprised to hear a woman speaking English in the room above me. I was even more startled when she was brought down into the cellar, and I realized she was one of the new hostages.

The guards abandoned their plans to call us by nicknames, and instead we were assigned numbers to keep our identities a secret; I was 10, Robert was 7, Hussein was 5, and Florence was 6.

Florence did as our captors directed and did not try to talk to Robert or me, while her translator, Hussein, filled in the hours with his constant prayers. The guards allowed the steady prayers from Hussein, but on occasion they would lift the door open and tell him to be quiet whenever they were nervous that American troops might be in the neighborhood.

One morning, when the guards took Hussein out for his bathroom break, he did not return immediately, and neither did Florence after her break. They were upstairs for an unusually long time, but I didn't hear any noise, so I assumed they were okay.

When they returned, Florence told me that the guards and Omar had forced her and her translator to make a video reading a transcript the kidnappers had written out for them on paper. I asked her if her statement was written in French, and she said they had written it in English. They didn't understand French and didn't want her to say any words they didn't understand. Hussein told me he pleaded in Arabic for his family to help him and for the government to pay his ransom before they killed him.

Omar and the guards would brag to us that women were always treated better in their Muslim culture than in the Christian world—when they weren't beating Florence, that is. The forty-four-year-old woman had been kidnapped from the Al-Jadriya district near Baghdad University during the first half of January. In addition to covering the wars in Afghanistan and Kosovo, she had written a book about the genocide in Rwanda.

During her first interrogation by the kidnappers, Florence told them she was married. Actually, they *asked* her if she was married because of the ring she wore on her left hand whenever she was sent on assignment in Arab countries. A married woman tends to get more respect from soldiers and contractors, Florence explained to me later. But when it came time for the kidnappers to assemble her ransom package, they took her back upstairs and interrogated her again. They wanted her husband's name and telephone number to demand money in exchange for her release.

Florence later told me she had a boyfriend, but she was afraid that if they called him and he told the kidnappers they were not married, she would be beaten by the guards. So she came clean and told the guards she was a single woman.

It sounded like all hell had broken loose in the room above me. Omar had a screaming fit and ordered all of the senior men in the group to convene their own shari'a court (shari'a is a legal system based on Islamic beliefs). After questioning and cross-questioning for several hours, they sent Florence out of the room while they deliberated her guilt or innocence.

It only took a few minutes for her jury to find her guilty of lying, and they told her if she did it again, they would kill her. Then they beat her. She had bruises all over her back and shoulders when they brought her back down into the hole.

But sometimes they gave her special privileges. For example, there were occasions when they would take her upstairs to have lunch with the woman of the house, and they would allow her to watch television, but Arabic programs only; they never allowed her to watch news programs.

It appeared as if Omar was serious about letting her out of there alive if they secured her ransom. Often he told her it was important that she write only good things about her time in captivity and of her captors when she was released. The cluelessness of our captors flabbergasted Florence. They beat her, starved her, kept her tied up like an animal—*and* they wanted her to be sure and write good things about them when she was released! I asked her what she told them she would write, and she laughed and said that of course she assured Omar only kind words would spill from her pen. After all, any other answer would have probably resulted in another beating for her. It was difficult for us to grasp just how credulous these men were.

One morning Florence returned from breakfast with the woman of the house, and she was carrying a Koran written in English that one of the guards had given her to read. I had heard Florence ask for something to read and was surprised to see they had actually granted her request. When they served us our lunch meal, I asked the guard if I could have something to read as well. He told me I could also have a Koran, but that mine would be written in Arabic. (The guards never did believe me when I said I did not speak Arabic. As it turned out, they never gave me a Koran written in Arabic or English.)

Later that evening, I could hear the guards upstairs watching one of their favorite shows, *America's Funniest Home Videos*. I could hear the audience laughing. A little girl had done something wrong, and to get out of trouble she said, "Oh, Mommy, I love you," and that was the video that won the hundred-thousand-dollar prize that night.

As I drifted off to sleep, I wondered if anyone was going to pay my twelve-million-dollar ransom.

••••

When Robert and I were first taken to the farm, there were no stairs leading down into the cellar, and the guards would have to hoist us up out of the hole for our twice-daily bathroom breaks, then lower us back down into the hole. But they tired of the bathroom chores after a few weeks and built metal stairs so that Robert and I could walk out on our own. Although our feet were untied to leave the hole, our hands were still tied and our masks covered our faces.

It was mid-February when the guards decided they needed a more secure path to enter the cellar. The guards were afraid that with our numbers growing, we might attack them and break free.

Before the new doorway was completed, the guards brought in two new hostages: an older man in his seventies and a younger man in his thirties. They were only with us for about three days; I guessed their ransom must have been paid. While they were there, the old man cried all three nights and kept asking for something in Arabic. I'm not sure what he was asking for—it could have been some kind of medication, but whatever it was, he never got it.

The new doorway was a big, noisy project that lasted for about a week. The guards were around us all the time, and we dared not move around or even stretch our muscles. They tore up the floor inside the house above us and then tunneled down alongside the cellar wall and lined it with walls of concrete. Then they broke through the cellar wall and installed a cage door with bars, like something you would see in a jail cell. That way, the guards could jump down into our hole behind the safety of an iron-bar door to bring us food, or to move us in and out for bathroom breaks. The new door had two loops for padlocks, and whenever we heard the locks being removed, we knew something was going to happen: a feeding, a bathroom break, or an interrogation and beating.

I smiled underneath my mask when the guard Hamid justified the new prison door as a path to regular meals, because the guards neglected to feed us much during the entire project. When we spoke up and said that we were hungry, the guards said too bad, they were too tired from building the new door to feed us.

19

CARRIE'S DIARY

Because they knew the U.S. government didn't pay ransoms, the kidnappers asked my Saudi Arabian employer to pay. The Saudi Arabia Trading and Construction Company negotiated with the gang for several months but did not have the twelve million dollars that the kidnappers demanded. Instead, the company offered to pay one million dollars. The gang refused to accept this and insisted on the higher figure. The FBI sent an agent fluent in Arabic to the company offices in Riyadh to help with the negotiations, and he was there assisting the entire time negotiations were going on with the gang.

At least I was still getting paid, and the checks were directly deposited into my bank account back home. I had put both Amanda's and Carrie's names on my account so they could access my money in case of emergency, and this was definitely an emergency. But there was a glitch: Carrie didn't have my password and spent weeks wrangling through red tape before she was able to access my account to make my car and house payments.

Carrie wrote in her diary on February 18 that she only had two dollars in her bank account, and I had six hundred dollars. "I created a budget for my sister and I for the future, neither of us are very good with money," she wrote.

Robert's wife, Ivy, called Carrie that day; she had a lot of questions, but mostly she wanted to know if Carrie had any new information.

"I could hear sadness in her voice," Carrie said later. The rest of her entry for that day continued:

Peter Cleveland from the office of California Senator Dianne Feinstein met with the FBI (along with Dianne) and said they were pleased with the investigation that the FBI is doing. He also told the FBI that they have gone way too far with their level of confidentiality.

Amanda and Kelly used to have lunch together all the time and hang out. My sister thought they were friends, so this has really hurt her. A new agent is being assigned to my sister. Someone from the FBI just had her sign some type of "funeral papers." Supposedly, these papers are not indicative that the FBI has any new information.

Bandar now e-mails and calls us frequently. He is providing a little more information than before. My mom told him that the FBI said he might be one of the kidnappers. This pissed Bandar off. Bandar suspects that the kidnappers are now speaking directly to the FBI. Of course, the FBI would not tell us this or anything else that would resemble information. Peter Cleveland said that he has a full security clearance, and that after hearing everything that the FBI has, it is okay to talk to Bandar and that he is not a bad guy. Originally, the FBI had told us not to speak to Bandar or anyone else from the company. We would get in trouble if we did. For example, we would be threatened to be "cut off from the investigation." Also, a guilt trip was placed on me that by talking to anyone from the company, [it] could disrupt the investigation and affect the prosecution of the kidnappers. Bandar was told not to speak to us or give us any information.

All of this was an effort by the FBI to control us and to keep us from getting information for whatever reason. We were told we did not have the "security clearance" to receive any information about Dad's investigation.

I smelled a pipe yesterday—reminded me of Dad and when he let me try a pipe when I was little. I'm dreaming of Dad every night. Usually good dreams.

On February 26, Carrie's journal entry began with a poem:

The Forgotten One

No one remembers you,
When you are suffering and in pain.
Only when you're in the spotlight
At the pinnacle of fortune and fame.
Locked up in chains,
Held by a gun
No one remembers
The forgotten one.
We laugh and focus
On weather, clothing trends and celebrities,
And things that are fun.
I heard him crying
Deep in the night.
I feel his pain
Though he is out of sight.
I will keep trying
To keep up the fight
Out from the darkness

And into the light.
I will tell others
Of my father's plight
So he is forgotten no more,
And his situation is made right.

By Carrie Cooper

February 27: Bandar called my cell phone today at 9:00 a.m. My cell does not usually work when I am at home, so it did not ring. It just made a noise that I had a message. Bandar has been trying to get a hold of me, but between schoolwork, my private practice, work, etc., we haven't had time to connect. When Bandar left his message today, he said that the kidnappers still have not contacted him since the one time that they did after the video was released. Not good news. This makes me sad.

Her entries for March continued:

I got a tattoo today. It is a Chinese symbol of love on the back of my ankle. When I got it, I was thinking of all of the people I love, including my Dad. The Chinese character reminds me of Hong Kong when I was younger and my family was intact. My Dad was okay and I was a little girl. Looking at this tattoo actually feels reassuring and soothing in a way because of the things it reminds me of.

My mom has been trying to call Jesse Jackson for weeks now to see if he is doing anything for my Dad like he said he would. He won't even return her phone calls. I've never even spoken to Jesse. My mom has also contacted Arnold S. (the governor's) office, and he said he would not get involved and "go against the government" or something to that effect. She also contacted Hillary Clinton's office, who did not want to get involved either.

March 18: Jenny Foo from the State Department called and left a message on my voice mail saying there is no new information about my Dad since the video, but they are still looking for him—no new leads.

This makes me very sad.

March 19: Ivy, Robert's wife, called me around 2:00 p.m. She had not seen Robert's video that was released recently. I haven't seen it either. But there is a woman my mom is talking to that is supposed to send my mom a copy. I told Ivy to call my mom on her cell because she is in Memphis, and that I'm sure my mom could send her a copy. Ivy sounded sad and frustrated. She said that she wasn't sure that the Philippine government was even negotiating for Robert. I told her I believed they were. I didn't tell her so, because I didn't want to make her feel bad, but I think the United States and the Philippines are doing a lot more to get Robert released than my dad. It's ironic, though, that Ivy and my family both feel as though our government is not doing enough or anything at all. She kept repeating how long Robert had been gone and how she wasn't sure if the kidnappers had postponed Robert's execution. We tried to believe everything was being done to find Roy and Robert, but we had no concrete proof of any actions by government agencies.

20

THE ROMANIANS

The guards brought four more hostages into our already crowded cellar: Romanian Prima TV reporter Marie Jeanne Ion; her camera-man, Sorin Mişcoci; and a reporter for the newspaper *Romania Libera*, named Ovidiu Ohanesian. The kidnappers had also taken hostage the Romanians' translator and tour guide, an Iraqi-American named Mohammad Munaf.

The sound of ripping masking tape sent a chill down my spine as it signaled that the guards were once again going to rob me of any physical comfort I had left. Hamid ordered me to sit up with my back against the wall, and he began wrapping the tape over the ski mask and around my eyes and ears. He cut the ties from my wrists, and for a brief instant I wondered if they were going to lead me out of the hole to my execution.

But instead, Hamid pushed my knees up to my chest and taped my arms to my thighs. Because it was so overcrowded in the hole, there was not enough room for all of us to lie down, so they taped me sitting up to allow more space for the new hostages.

After Hamid secured my arms to my legs, he began hitting me in the head. "Stay right here. Do not talk, do not look, or we will kill you," he commanded. "We will come back in the morning to move you."

I thought there was no way I could survive taped up like that for eight hours. Thankfully, the guards came back into our hole just three hours later, and after a lengthy discussion in Arabic, they cut the tape back off my arms and legs, allowing me to stretch back out, and retied my hands in front of me.

"Do not move," Hamid again ordered. "We will make more room tomorrow."

They did so by moving Yasser Obati to a different location. The guards told Amar his seventeen-year-old son was being taken to an old factory, where he would be held hostage with another Iraqi his own age.

Amar threw a fit and demanded that Yasser remain with us. The guards had beaten Yasser several times, and Amar was afraid his teenage son would be taken away and tortured. The guards told Amar his son would be released when the ransoms were paid for both of them. If the ransoms were not paid, they said Yasser would be killed and his body chopped up and dumped in his mother's yard. Even though Amar and Yasser were Sunnis, they were not Wahhabi Sunnis, like our captors, and were therefore treated worse than the non-Muslims. Amar cried for hours after his son was taken away.

I wasn't sure if the Romanians had no fear or if they were just plain crazy. The guards warned them not to talk to each other or they would be killed, but they started chatting away before the guards even closed the door. They were talking so loud I was sure the guards could hear them and would come back downstairs to beat them, but they didn't. Like our Arab captors, the Romanians didn't do rules very well.

In addition to her native language, Marie spoke Arabic; some of the others could also speak French. One night after I heard Marie talking to Florence in English, I finally spoke to the group. There were now ten of us held hostage in the cellar: Robert and myself, Florence and Hussein, Amar and Yasser, the three Romanians, and Munaf.

The reporters were in Baghdad to cover Romanian president Traian B sescu's visit on Easter Sunday, with Romanian troops deployed here for the war. They had been kidnapped March 26 on a street near the Flowerland Hotel (in the Al-Jadriya district) where they were staying. Three vehicles suddenly surrounded their car, and the kidnappers jumped out with AK-47s and pulled the Romanians and their Iraqi guide out of their car and into the getaway vehicles.

The Romanians told us they were taken to a house where they were kept for about three days. Their guards had actually bragged that two other kidnapping gangs were looking for them, saying that our captors were the best in the racket because they got to the Romanians and their guide first.

The newcomers described the house and their treatment to me, and it was clear I was never held at this safe house. Their hands and feet were never tied; they were locked inside a bedroom, where they were provided foam mattresses and blankets, and they were fed regularly. When they were moved, they were told they were being taken to a new location where they would receive better treatment and meals. Instead, they were brought to Robert and me in our underground prison.

The ten of us were very cramped in the small space and barely had room to lie down. When the guards fed us, we would sit in a circle and they would bring a tray of food and set it in front of us, then hand us plates to dip up some rice. We weren't allowed to lift up our masks to eat, but we could tilt our head backs to look underneath and down at our food.

The guards only used one little tin cup to give us water. The guard, usually Hamid, would pass the cup to one of us, fill it from a water pitcher (but only about halfway), then pass the cup on to the next person. Luckily, none of us got sick sharing germs with one another.

As holidays approached, I would get nervous that the guards would abandon their efforts to find someone to pay my ransom and instead sacrifice me for the insurgency's cause in a videotaped beheading. I had survived Thanksgiving, Christmas, New Year—and now Easter approached.

And with spring came the rain. It didn't rain that often in Iraq. There were usually a couple of rainfalls in November, but the rainy season, such as it is, comes in March and April.

This is when I learned that the room above us did not have a solid roof, but a palm-leaf roof, like the critter shack Robert and I had been held in months earlier. We had one drenching rainstorm that dumped buckets of water into the house, and it flowed right through the holes in the floor into our cellar below. It occurred to me that if our room flooded, we would be trapped and could possibly drown. I remembered asking God to send rain as a signal I would survive my ordeal just days after I was kidnapped. I was now praying to God to please stop the rain.

This is the front of the house where we were held. Though you can't tell it from this shot, the house had a palm-leaf roof. When it rained, it would fill our underground cell with buckets of water.

Not long after the Romanians joined us, the guards started a mysterious and loud project upstairs. I could hear a lot of banging of metal and wondered what in the world they were up to now. This went on for about a week—the noise of hammering and pounding on metal. The sounds of metal on metal sent my imagination reeling. I remembered seeing the videotape of British national Kenneth Bigley after he was kidnapped. He was wearing an orange jumpsuit inside a small metal cage with his knees pulled to his chest as he pleaded for his life. American forces found his lifeless body sometime later. Zarqawi had beheaded him in a video.

I was afraid they were building a cage for a new video.

But when they brought the metal object down into the cellar, it didn't sound like a cage; it sounded like a giant metal door. The guards moved us all against one wall, and then they started banging on the ceiling. After about two hours of talking and banging and the sounds of chains clanging, Robert and I were introduced to our new location in the cellar: iron beds made out of metal fencing. The guards hung the bed in midair by attaching chains to the rusty pipes around the ceiling above us.

My sleeping area in the cell.

I don't know why we were the ones chosen for what turned out to be the most uncomfortable, even painful, and sometimes suffocating position in the cellar. The whole setup was ridiculous. The guards helped us up on top of the swinging beds and told Robert and me to lie still and not make any noise or we would be punished. I missed sleeping on the concrete floor. At least sometimes they would give us a mat for the floor.

It was unbearable, especially as spring arrived and temperatures soon reached one hundred degrees in the cellar. At least the concrete floor below me was cool, but the top of our swinging cage door was the hottest part of the room. The worst part of that experience was the humidity. Water would condense on the rusty pipes, and the nasty, corroded fluids dripped down on us like a Chinese water torture.

Remaining still on the gate like the guards ordered was impossible. The steel mesh left indents in the skin, and whenever I rolled over, the metal on metal would squeak, and the chains that ran along the pipes would clang as it swung back and forth.

Time after time the guards would yell at me for moving. "You don't move! You make noise!" Hamid would shout. Sometimes he would beat me. I tried telling him I must have been rolling over in my sleep, but that didn't stop the beatings.

This went on for about two weeks, and then all of a sudden it was not that important to the guards if I moved or not. I guess beating me just became too much work for them. Nobody cared anymore.

Omar made a rare appearance at the farmhouse; I had come to learn that was never a good sign. He was there to confront Amar, whose family members could not get access to the family bank accounts or sell the house to secure his release.

Amar was gone for several hours. I could hear him screaming and crying in the room above us. Omar wanted to know how much money he had, how to access the bank accounts, even what kind of cars he drove. In order to get the information, he and the guards tortured Amar. They hung him upside down and shocked him using a 12-volt truck battery; plugged into anything as simple as a phone charger, it could deliver 120 volts of electricity. They shocked him on his chest, his arms, his legs, and his genitals for nearly two hours. Amar was so numb afterward, he could barely walk for at least three days when he was taken outside for a bathroom break.

We didn't trust anything the guards told us, and for a long time we could not trust each other. At times the guards would pull us out of the cellar individually for interrogations; they would ask if we knew who our fellow captors were and if we were talking to one another.

I talked to Hussein several times but never told him my name. The guards' threats to kill us if we talked seemed like one promise they might keep. I didn't want Hussein to suddenly blurt out my name if they tortured him, and my instincts were correct—Hussein was later tortured with the truck battery.

After Hussein's torture, I was taken outside to go to the bathroom, and Hamid started hitting me without warning and accused me of talking to the other hostages. I protested that I had not spoken to anyone, and I blamed the noise on Hussein's constant prayers.

As it turned out, Hussein's devotion and continual praying provided good cover for us to whisper to one another when we were sure the guards were sleeping, and we developed individual signals we would give to one another before starting a conversation. Months later, these signals probably saved my life.

Our hanging beds were on the opposite end of the room from the rusty metal stairs that led from the room above down into the cellar. Robert's bed was closest to the door. Underneath Robert on the cement floor was Amar, and the two Romanians lay next to him. Munaf was directly below me, and the two women were on the other side of the room, next to the stairs.

Whenever I wanted to talk to Munaf, I would reach down below me and touch him on his left shoulder. Munaf was having a hard time adjusting to captivity and cried every night. He seemed to be even more upset over his situation than the Romanians. I finally asked him what was wrong, as I was concerned that he could have been beaten and injured before the guards transferred him to our underground prison.

But Munaf wasn't worried about himself. His wife was eight months pregnant, and he was afraid that the stress of his kidnapping might lead her to miscarriage. He and his wife had one daughter, who was fourteen years old, and in the years since, they had tried to conceive another child, but his wife miscarried every time. Munaf said this was the first time it looked like she would carry the child to full term.

Munaf was Iraqi by birth but had obtained American citizenship and had once lived in New York. However, his family now lived in Romania, where Munaf operated a lumber business, an enterprise made successful by the rebuilding efforts of the Americans in Iraq. Most buildings in the Middle East are constructed of concrete or cinder blocks, as trees are scarce, but the Americans had a fondness for lumber, which they were using to build the Army bases. Munaf said his business was booming.

We talked about his family often, and then he would cry himself to sleep.

Amar would touch my hand when he wanted to talk, and I would reach down to touch Florence's wrist when I wanted to talk to her. One time, though, signals got crossed. We had just finished eating dinner, and as Hamid, the guard, cleared the plates, his hand accidentally grazed the wrist of Marie's cameraman, Sorin; it was his signal to begin a conversation with her.

"What do you want?" Sorin said as he pulled the mask up over his face, only to see Hamid squatting right in front of him.

The mistake earned him a slap across the face.

21

NO SMOKING

The Romanians were in a foul mood. They had been forced to make videos for the kidnappers, with guns pointed at their heads, while they demanded that the Romanian government withdraw its nearly nine hundred troops from Iraq. But they weren't as upset over troop withdrawals as they were over their own withdrawal from nicotine.

All three of the Romanian hostages had a cigarette habit—they were used to smoking about two packs a day. Now, all of a sudden, they had nothing to smoke. Needless to say, they were going nuts. They chattered nonstop, and although their hands and feet were tied up, they managed to fidget and kept gesturing wildly with their hands and arms whenever the guards were out of the room. The others were so close to me I could feel their every movement, because as they moved, they actually touched me.

At one point, the tobacco withdrawal became too much for the photographer; he pleaded with us to help him kill the guards and escape. "There are more of us than there are of them. The next time the guard comes with our food, we can kill him and get out of here," Sorin said.

"I suppose we could kill him," I replied, "but what happens when we go upstairs to face five or six other guards with AK-47s? And then what are we going to do even if we can take out all the gunmen—escape out of this compound into the countryside, where any number of the neighbors want to kill us? And what if we did find a car to escape? We would need the keys and directions to get to Baghdad. And what if we get stopped at an Iraqi police checkpoint? The crooked cops would most likely bring us right back here and collect a reward for our return. The odds of our escaping are not good."

That didn't seem to deter him. Sorin was determined to kill the guards in order to get a cigarette. And a beer—he and the other Romanians talked incessantly about having a glass of wine or a beer, and a smoke.

Sorin really wanted to kill those guards.

Florence offered that while we were not in the greatest of circumstances, at least we were all alive. If we overpowered the guard and went upstairs, we might not be alive for very long.

After about two weeks of suffering from tobacco withdrawal, the Romanians were coming out of their skins, and Marie finally confronted Omar. Since she spoke fluent Arabic, she convinced him to give the Romanians smoking privileges. The men would be allowed one cigarette a day when they were taken outside the hole in the morning for their bathroom break. Because Marie was a woman, and women were treated better in the Islamic world, she would be allowed two smokes a day, one at each bathroom break.

Two weeks into the smoking routine, one of the guards who frowned on Marie's smoking habit told her it was *haraam*, legally forbidden in their brand of Islam. He also said he was going to help her quit by cutting her back from two cigarettes a day to just one. But Marie was having none of that; her nerves were already at an end, and Omar had given his word that she would be allowed to have her two smoke breaks a day. She lost all control and started screaming at the guard in Arabic, threatening to tell Omar that the guard was not following his orders. Marie had learned enough about the culture to know that the guards would not dare to deviate from the boss's instructions on how the hostages were to be treated. Basically, she threatened to tell on him.

Marie was quite the negotiator, and she got her second cigarette right then and every day she was held in captivity. Her father—Vasile Ion, a Social Democratic Party senator—was not as successful when he demanded that Romanian president Traian B sescu recall his country's troops from Iraq in order to secure the release of his daughter.

Even with their nicotine habits fed, the Romanians were a chatty bunch. Most of us would wait until nighttime, when we were pretty sure the guards were sleeping, before starting a conversation. Signals were sent, then a few seconds later, a hushed exchange took place. I thought I heard Marie crying one night and tapped her on her shoulder to initiate a conversation. When I asked her what was wrong, Marie said she missed her mother.

We didn't fully trust one another; we had no way of knowing if someone would sell us out with the guards in exchange for better treatment. However, on May 1, the Orthodox Easter, the Romanians acknowledged the Christian holiday to one another in front of the Muslim hostages. "Christ has risen!" they said to each other in hushed tones. They could have made the sign of the cross with their hands tied, but they did not take the additional risk.

The Romanians mostly spoke to one another, but sometimes Marie would talk with Florence, and I had conversed with nearly everyone in the room. During this entire period, Robert only spoke once.

At one point, Robert's silence had finally gotten on Sorin's nerves, and he started pushing Robert, literally, as he lay there with his mask covering his face. Sorin asked Robert a lot of questions, such as who he was, why he didn't talk, how he was feeling. Finally, Robert sat up, pulled up his mask, and addressed the Romanian.

"We're not supposed to talk," Robert said, and with that, he pulled the mask back over his face and lay back down.

"What's the matter with him?" Sorin asked me.

"That's just how he copes; leave him alone," I responded.

Spring had turned into summer, and the temperature became unbearably hot. The humidity from our breathing filled the air and condensed on the rusty pipes above us, creating a constant misty rain of orange iron that coated our already sweaty skin.

The women were forced to wear a traditional long-sleeved Muslim overgarment called an *abaya*. The women were boiling underneath their heavy white cloaks. Often, though, the guards would untie Florence and Marie's hands, another gesture to show that women were treated better in Islam, and I learned later that the ladies would take advantage of this goodwill to take off the abayat whenever the guards were not around. It was blistering hot in our hole, and Marie developed a painful rash on her left shoulder. The fact that none of us had bathed in two months didn't help matters.

Underneath the abaya, the women wore a thin undershirt with spaghetti straps. The ladies were also wearing heavy jogging pants with shorts underneath, and would pull the pants down to their ankles and just wear their shorts in the room. Whenever they heard a noise indicating a guard was coming to the door, they quickly pulled the jogging pants back up, put the abayat back on, and replaced the masks back over their heads. But after a few weeks in the searing heat, the women refused to put the abayat back on when the guards appeared.

"You should wear this at all times, because in Islam women must always be covered when they are around men," one of the guards said.

Certainly women are supposed to be covered according to Islamic law, but also in Islamic law, women are not supposed to be kidnapped and held hostage in the same room with men they are not related to. Besides, the gang didn't make any sense in anything they ever said.

We men were allowed to remove our shirts, but that effort to stay cool was futile.

••••

As the weeks dragged on and the temperatures rose, Hussein began to tell me about his family. He was raised on an island in a river in northern Iraq. He actually fought against Saddam Hussein with the Kurds until the Iraqi police caught him. Hussein said he was used to being held captive, and that he had previously been imprisoned for about a year. He was released after signing a piece of paper that explained if he was ever caught fighting against his country or criticizing the Iraqi government, he would be killed.

A Shiite, Hussein would sometimes strike up a conversation with the Sunni guards about differences in their religion, and it always resulted in a physical whipping for him. I told Hussein he should stop engaging them in these religious discussions to avoid the beatings, but he was adamant. He said their beliefs about Islam were wrong and that he wanted to set them on the right path.

Needless to say, that never happened.

22

AIR-CONDITIONING

The attack of the sand fleas was agonizing.

The room above us must have been completely infested with the bugs from the guards constantly tracking sand into the house. And when the men shuffled their sandals over the floor, the sand would fall through the cracks, bringing with it the fleas to feast on the hostages underground.

The bloodsucking vermin were impossible to squash as they bit our hands and ankles, our backs, and our faces, and the itching was relentless. There was a constant chorus of slapping, scratching, and cursing in English, French, Arabic, and Romanian. Robert scratched in silence. We begged our guards for some bug spray to keep the pests off of us, or some medicated lotion to treat the rash of bites all over our bodies. The guards gave us their word they would bring us some lotion to treat the oozing wounds, but they never delivered on their promise.

The others pleaded with our captors to take us out of the hole for a bath; they had not had a bath or shower in two to four months. The last time I'd had a chance to bathe was in April, my second opportunity in captivity. First they took me outside for a haircut, using a little electric razor that was set on the lowest setting it could go; the guard gave me a buzz cut that left my hair about an eighth of an inch long. Then they took me back into the main house, where there was a bathroom and a garden hose used for a shower. The guards told me I could remove my mask when they left, reminding me that when they returned, I should stay where I was and pull my mask back down over my face.

The shower was a huge relief, but I did not anticipate the additional grooming by the guards. While the Wahhabi Sunni do not shave their faces, they do shave their armpits, and when the guards came back into the bathroom, one on each side of me, I could see the razor underneath my mask. It was the kind of razor my grandfather used, a double-edged safety razor; you twist the bottom of the handle to open the razor head, then drop in the razor and twist the handle to close it. It's not a steady tool; even though it's covered with metal, the blade is still wobbly and can easily cut delicate skin.

One of the guards lifted my right arm while the other guard shaved my armpit; then they moved to my other side to shave under my left arm. I was somewhat surprised that the guards were grooming me to their religious standards. And I was hopeful, ever so hopeful, that they would stop at the armpits—because Sunnis also shave the pubic hairs from their private parts.

I was thinking, *No way. No way will they do that to me.*

I was wrong.

One guard bent down in front of me and started shaving me. But this was way too intimate, and he didn't finish; instead, he stood up and said something to the other guard in Arabic. Thankfully, it was too intimate for him as well, and he took my hand and gave me the razor and told me to finish. The men walked behind me so I could lift my mask to see what I was doing, but not what they looked like, and I did what I was told. It seemed like a small price to pay. Then they gave me some new clothes to put on and left the room.

These guys are nuts, I thought.

But a shower sounded great right now, and the guards finally agreed. They took us out of the hole one at a time before the sun rose, and after our bathroom break outside, they literally hosed us down with a garden hose. But just the men, not the women. Eventually, the guards built a little room upstairs about the size of a closet and ran the garden hose through it, where the women (and eventually us men) were allowed to shower about every six weeks.

Florence decided one time to shock the guards, and after her shower she put on her underclothes and then charged out of the shower closet door, demanding more towels. The guards panicked and hid their faces, yelling, "*Haraam, haraam!*" I could hear the guards running around the room, telling her to get back into the shower and they would bring her more towels. This time the guards kept their word.

It also looked as if the guards were going to keep their word to bring an air conditioner down into our hole. Marie was the first to tell us about it, but I didn't believe her until the guards came into our hole and installed an electrical plug. It was several days before the guards brought a portable air conditioner into the hole, plugged it in, and turned it on—within seconds, our hellhole turned into complete heaven. The humidity dissipated in the cool air, and at last my skin felt dry, not slimy. I felt I could breathe for the first time in months.

Like I said, it was sheer heaven. For about three minutes. Then the air conditioner suddenly shut down, and all of the lights in the house above us went dark. The generator was silent.

The guards came storming down the stairs into the hole; we could hear them kicking and pounding on the machine and jabbering in Arabic. After a long discussion the guards left the room, and I asked Mohammad Munaf to translate the conversation. He said the guards thought they needed bigger fuses.

The air conditioner fiasco lasted for at least a month. Marie was always hopeful the unit would be fixed any day, but I told her it had taken three months to get a 5-watt light installed in our hole, so I was not optimistic about the air-conditioning.

But they kept trying. The guards would work on the wiring, start up the generator, and then plug in the air conditioner. It would work for about thirty glorious seconds, then shut down, taking all the electricity in the house with it. The guards abandoned the project for about a week, leaving the nonworking machine in the middle of the room as a cruel reminder of what we were missing. After we complained, the guards gave it another try and plugged in the machine and turned it on. The air conditioning came on with a roar, but after about a minute it conked out with a whimper. This scene repeated itself over and over again, like a scene from the movie *Groundhog Day*, and after about a month, the guards just gave up on the air-conditioning project. When I asked them what the problem was, Hamid said they had purchased two air conditioners, one for the guards upstairs and one for our cellar, but the generator would only support one system.

Someone had to make a sacrifice, and we were the ones chosen.

However, the noise from the generator and the hum of the air conditioner above us, along with the nonstop praying by Hussein, gave us ample cover to talk to one another.

Food was often the topic of conversations: how little we were being served by the guards, the food we ate back home, and so forth. The guards started bringing fruit, bananas, tomatoes, and sometimes cucumbers, but most of the time it was already rotting. I had not brushed my teeth in at least five months, and I started using the stems from the banana peels as a toothbrush. I have always taken meticulous care of my teeth. The banana peel, as it turned out, worked fairly well as a substitute toothbrush.

I told Florence about Memphis barbecue and catfish. It turns out they don't eat catfish in France, but Florence had read about fried catfish in books about the South and was eager to learn about the regional delicacy. Even though most catfish consumed these days is raised on catfish farms in stocked ponds, it still has a mild gamey taste to it, very different from other fish.

I told her about some really nutty people back home in Memphis who hunt for catfish along the Mississippi River. I say hunt rather than fish because they usually don't use poles; instead, they look for water holes near the banks and reach into the hole to pull out the catfish (which are known to lurk in the muddy water beneath) by hand. But sometimes, instead of a catfish, you might find yourself pulling up a poisonous water moccasin. I've fished for catfish using a pole from the back of a boat, but I was never crazy enough to try and pull one out of the water with my hands.

Florence was fascinated with the South and had a romantic, if sometimes not-always-accurate impression of the region. She also asked me who I thought would run for president after Bush's term expired. I thought it was funny that Bush had just been reelected, and already people were talking about who would replace him.

I told her that Senator Hillary Clinton would probably run, as well as Secretary of State Colin Powell. I didn't know, of course, that Powell had stepped down just two months after I was kidnapped. Powell was the first African-American to hold that position, and the first to serve as chairman of the Joint Chiefs of Staff.

Florence asked me if I thought a black man could win the presidency in the United States, and I said yes, I think he could. "But you are from the South," she said. "You would vote for a black man?" I told her yes, I would vote for Colin Powell.

Elections were still a long way off in France as well, but Florence told me there was a potential candidate running who, if elected, would be the first non-Catholic to preside over the country in centuries. Catholicism was a deal breaker for the French, and Florence said people were not sure whether to vote for him. That made me chuckle. I told her that when Kennedy was running for president in 1960, I remember my dad saying he would be the first Catholic ever elected and people then did not know whether they could trust him.

We talked about the war in Iraq. Florence said there was no Al-Qaeda in Iraq until American troops arrived, and complained that we never did find any weapons of mass destruction. I agreed there was no Al-Qaeda before we got there, but they were here now, and we needed to defeat the terrorists. I've never been very political, but I am a patriot.

Moving on to a safer topic, I told her I had never been to France, but that when I stood on the banks of the Mississippi River, I could see what used to be France's western empire on the other side. That is, until Napoleon Bonaparte sold it to Thomas Jefferson in 1803 for about twenty-three million dollars. Florence had never heard of the Louisiana Purchase, which included territory that would become more than a dozen states, including Arkansas, which lies on the other side of the Mississippi River from Tennessee. Bonaparte needed the money to finance his military activities in Europe, and in exchange, America got complete control of the ports in New Orleans and the Mississippi River all the way to Canada.

Florence talked about cooking, and one recipe in particular, a pork loin with mustard sauce. When I asked if she made it with Dijon mustard, she seemed insulted and responded that no other kind of mustard existed. Then she told me the differences between French butter and butter in America and how the French version has a far superior flavor and doesn't burn as easily. Of course, it also has more fat in it and less water than American butter; the fat content of French butter is actually regulated by law.

I told her about the world-famous Corky's Ribs and Bar-B-Q restaurant back home on Poplar Avenue, a family business that is renowned for its sauces and seasonings. The ribs were a favorite of Elvis Presley's and of mine. They rub the ribs with a mix of paprika, salt, garlic, and other secret spices, and the results are good eating.

We also talked about her ransom. The guards were telling her they were going to let her go soon, but I told her not to get her hopes up too much—by this time, the guards had told me at least five times they were going to release me.

I really enjoyed my conversations with Florence, and I told her when we did manage to get out of that place, I wanted her to come to Memphis to visit me and I would introduce her to barbecue, catfish, and old France. She still hasn't taken me up on my offer, but I hope someday she will. I have a lot to thank her for, including her part in my eventual rescue.

23

MUNAF

The Romanian hostages and Munaf were taken out of the room one at a time. I never saw them again. My careful noting of the passage of time told me it was May 23, and the guards told me that the Romanian government paid the journalists' ransom, Munaf's family had paid his ransom, and that they were all released.

I later learned that the guards had told me the truth—the Romanians and Munaf were indeed safe and free after nearly two months in captivity. Four million dollars was asked for their release, and reportedly was paid.

Other than tobacco withdrawal, the Romanians handled their captivity with some ease, having ignored all death threats concerning speaking to one another, and I admired Marie's spunk in standing up to Omar and the guards to demand daily cigarette breaks.

Ovidiu Ohanesian later told the Associated Press that our guards had been civil in their treatment of us but described our conditions as harsh. "We spent 51 days underground, crowded in a small cellar, a weak light bulb and blindfolded," Ohanesian said. "There was no air, I was sweating abundantly, worse than a sauna."[1]

The Romanians' tour guide, Iraqi-American Munaf, did not fare as well. Munaf had cried a lot and seemed truly miserable and afraid of our captors. That's why I was completely surprised to later discover that Munaf was accused of plotting the Romanians' kidnapping.

One week after Munaf and the Romanians were released, Munaf was indicted in absentia by the Romanian government on May 30 as a conspirator in their kidnapping and soon found himself being held captive again, only this time by the Multi-National Force–Iraq, which is the U.S.-led military command in charge of the Iraq war. Munaf was taken into custody and charged with committing hostile or warlike acts in Iraq—specifically, the kidnappings of Sorin Mişcoci, Ovidiu Ohanesian, and Marie Jeanne Ion.

Munaf was said to be in cahoots with Omar Hayssam, a Syrian businessman who lived in Romania. Hayssam was under investigation for various criminal activities, and his bank accounts had been frozen. Munaf and Hayssam were charged with scheming to lure Marie and her colleagues to Iraq, kidnap them, and then demand four million dollars in ransom. Hayssam would volunteer to pay the ransom from his frozen account. That way, he could recover his money and look like a hero at the same time.

While they were still in captivity, Marie got into an argument with Munaf; she started yelling at him, saying they would not be in their current situation if he had not brought them to Iraq. I defended Munaf; I told Marie she should be mad at the guards, not Munaf.

Turns out, Marie was correct after all.

After the Romanians were released, Florence was told her negotiations were on track and that she would be released soon. Omar also told her that if she published anything negative about the kidnappers, the remaining hostages would suffer. In return for her silence, Omar promised to give Florence a television set, and surprisingly enough, he actually delivered.

It was late at night when Hamid came down into our hole with the portable TV. Florence was closest to the trapdoor, and I was on the other side of the room; Hamid told us the television was only to be watched by hostage number six, meaning Florence. Hamid told her she could not watch any news; to the rest of us, he said, "No talking, no looking."

Hamid sat with Florence as she pulled up her mask to watch some sort of Arabic soap opera on television; I was trying to sleep and wasn't paying much attention. He only let her watch for about fifteen minutes before he turned it off and went back upstairs. Hamid warned Florence not to turn the TV back on, but she ignored him.

I didn't notice at first, what with Hussein just a few inches away from me, bowing and praying, but the guards heard it. The door to the cellar slammed open, and Hamid came running down inside. In a split second he grabbed the television and slapped Florence hard across the face.

"No look, no look!" he screamed.

Florence protested and said that Omar said it was okay for her to watch, but Hamid hit her again.

Then he saw Hussein, mid-bow in prayer.

"You look, you look!" Hamid shouted, thinking that Hussein was watching the television with Florence. The guard retied Hussein's hands behind his back and beat him so ferociously that he knocked one of the man's teeth out of his head.

Hamid crossed back to Florence and pounded her with his fists until she screamed out in pain; then he took the television set and left. That was the last time Florence was allowed to watch Arabic soap operas.

After Hamid left the room, I crawled over to where Florence was sitting and quietly asked if she was okay. She said that she was, and that she only screamed because that's what the guard wanted to hear. "If you scream, they will go away," she said.

I then asked Hussein if he was okay. He said yes, but his face was bruised and swollen. He lay there quietly for a few minutes and then resumed praying.

With the Romanians gone and more room in the cell for those of us left, the guards moved Robert and me off of the swinging iron beds and back down onto the floor. It was much cooler, and with fewer people breathing, the humidity dropped significantly.

Omar came for a visit that afternoon. Usually a dreadful experience, this time his actions were quite unexpected. Hopeful, even. He actually apologized to Florence for the beating Hamid had delivered to her and Hussein. Hamid had overreacted, and Omar said he would be fired for his actions. Omar seemed to be afraid that the attack would cause Florence to write nasty articles about him once she was released. He asked her again to write good things about the gang, and gracious Florence said but *of course* she would write nice things about him.

Hamid was fired that night, replaced with another man whose name we were told was Muslim. Muslim was easier to deal with. He didn't beat everyone, like Hamid; he would just bring us our food. Sometimes he would talk to Amar in Arabic. Once in a while he would sit by me and pat me on the leg and talk to me.

"You have been here for a very long time," Muslim said at the outset of our first conversation. "We are trying to negotiate so you can get out of here."

"I hope the negotiations are going well," I responded.

What Hamid had not seemed to understand was that while our religions were different (and in his mind, inferior), we still had worth. Literally. Florence learned her worth after sharing a lunch with the woman of the house upstairs in the kitchen. She always wore her mask when she ate, but when she heard the sound of footsteps approaching, she recognized the swaggering steps of Omar.

The Sunni told Florence he had been shopping in the market and bought her a gift that he said reminded him of the French journalist. Omar took her hand and gave her a garment, and told the woman of the house to lead Florence to the shower closet to change clothes.

Florence couldn't wait to show me her new present after the guards led her back into our hole. It was underwear—a white linen one-piece, with thin straps that looked like a bathing suit. It was decorated with fake euro bills. Sure, the apparel reminded Omar of Florence! Florence meant money. All of us hostages meant money—money for the insurgency.

24

ANOTHER RANSOM PAID

The temperature in our cell climbed well over 120 degrees, signaling the arrival of June and marking my seventh month in captivity.

The guards were telling Florence that negotiations for her release with the French government were going well, but I was skeptical. The guards had told me my release was imminent on several occasions, but here I was, still. The kidnappers were asking several million dollars for her release—an outrageous amount of money.

"You might be released tomorrow; you might get out of here in another three months," I whispered to her. Florence said she understood, and resigned herself to wait it out, to survive day by day like the rest of us.

But just in case the guards were being truthful with Florence, I decided to take an enormous risk and tell her who I was so that in her debriefing afterward with the army, police, or officials with the French government, she could tell them I was still alive.

"My name is Roy Hallums," I told Florence. "The other man being held with us—who has not spoken—is Robert Tarongoy. We work for the Saudi Arabia Trading and Construction Company. We were kidnapped from the Mansour district in Baghdad on November 1."

Just days later, on June 11, the guards came into our dank pit to bring us lunch, and they took Florence and her translator out of the cellar without a word to us as to what was about to happen. Since the guards had told Florence on three or four occasions that week that she would be released soon, I started to wonder if today was her lucky day.

The guards brought us our meals at dinnertime, and as they took us outside afterward for our bathroom break, they also removed the thin floor mats used by Florence and Hussein. I suspected that this meant her ransom had been paid and that they'd been released.

Amar managed to confirm it. While being served our dinner a few nights later, he struck up a conversation in Arabic with the guard, and I distinctly heard the word *Florence*. After the guard collected our dishes and left, I scooted over to Amar and tapped him on the hand to begin a conversation. When he responded by touching my ankle, I asked if Florence's trade had gone okay and whether they were really released.

"Yes," Amar said. "Omar drove them to Baghdad, and the exchange went well." One of the guards later told me the French government paid six million dollars for her release, but French officials denied any ransom was paid.

Florence kept her word and did not reveal any of the torture or beatings delivered by Omar and the gang. He had warned her that if she criticized them in any way, the remaining hostages would suffer for it. Florence knew all too well the barbaric methods of the gang, so while she fully cooperated in the debriefing by French government officials, she revealed little to the public.

The *Guardian* newspaper in London reported, "The editorial director at *Libération*, Antoine de Gaudemar, said the journalist apparently suffered no ill treatment or harassment while in captivity."[1]

Time magazine said Florence downplayed her ordeal and declined to discuss other hostages with whom she was held, citing security concerns. "And she insists she shouldn't be regarded as a role model: 'when you live through something so publicly, it becomes a communal story. People who recognize me, congratulate me, it's a little funny. Was I really a hero? For me, a hero is someone who leads a fight, gloriously, with a firm stand. I didn't fight for anything. I was captured, held and delivered. I was an object,'" *Time* reported.[2]

Marie paid homage to Florence in an interview with Romanian TV the day after Florence was released and said that her fellow journalist was remarkable throughout her ordeal. "She constantly encouraged us. She never allowed us to give up hope that we would be released," Marie said.

"Her abduction transformed Ms. Aubenas into a rallying figure for press freedom advocates in France and beyond," the BBC said. "The Paris-based group Reporters Without Borders worked tirelessly towards her release. Her picture and that of Mr. Saadi hung on walls in cities across Europe. French broadcasters regularly reminded viewers that the two remained in captivity. The campaign increased pressure on the government to do everything to secure her release—as it had done last year with two other French reporters captured in Iraq."[3]

What little Florence did say publicly still angered Omar, who told Amar he was so infuriated by her comments that he actually called the French embassy to complain! Omar told the French officials that if they did not stop Florence from saying "bad things" about the group, he would make a lot of trouble for the French in Iraq. It was his typical blustering with nothing to back it up. I thought about the French official on the other end of the phone, who must have wondered what kind of crazy person he was talking to.

A week after Florence was released, Amar was called out of the room by Omar and told to write a letter to his family. Omar was aggravated that Amar's family had not sold his two houses, his truck, or emptied his bank account to free him and Yasser.

Omar was a conservative Muslim who believed that the men in the family should own all of the property and control access to money, but somehow he could not grasp the reality that Amar's wife could not pay the ransom without her husband's permission, and his presence.

After Amar was finished with his letter, I was also taken out of the underground room, and Omar told me to write a letter to my family, specifically, my daughters and my sister, to ask for help in meeting the kidnappers' ransom demands.

> *June 18, 2005*
>
> *My name is Roy Hallums.*
> *I live in Memphis, Tennessee.*
> *My mother's name was Aline.*
> *I went to school at Memphis State University and graduated in 1972.*
> *I am requesting that my family help me in any way possible. My life is in danger and I need help from anyone to get out of this situation. Please help as soon as you can.*
>
> *Roy Hallums*

I'm not sure to whom the kidnappers sent the letter, but it was the FBI who relayed it to my family.

Carrie was frustrated with the FBI and was refusing to return their phone calls, so the FBI called Susan to convey to her that they had some new information and that it was very important that Carrie meet with them. When Susan asked to attend the meeting with Carrie, the agent told her she was not invited.

"I was frantic," Susan said. "I was afraid they might bring horrific news for Carrie, and I knew that she would need me there for support. Carrie lived about fifty miles away from me, and in rush hour traffic it could take as long as an hour and a half for me to drive over to the Westminster area. So I asked the FBI agent if I should already be near her house when they delivered whatever news they had, but they wouldn't even answer my question. I told them they were being ridiculous and asked them what they would do if it were their child." She continued, "I was in tears by that point, it seemed like they were just trying to make our ordeal even more terrible than it already was."

On the day of the meeting, Susan decided to make the drive over to Carrie's house just in case they were there to tell her I was dead. Susan was about halfway there when Carrie called her on her cell phone and told her about the letter.

"Carrie was crying. She told me about the letter, and she was furious that the agents would not allow her to have a copy of it," Susan said.

Carrie memorized the letter as best she could. Susan was frustrated that she was not allowed to look at it. After all, I wrote her hundreds of letters during my twenty years of service in the Navy—who better to verify it was my handwriting than Susan?

"Carrie was suffering so much, and this was just one more encounter for her to endure," Susan said. "I felt that our lives might never be the way it was before November 1. It seemed like this would never end. Day after day we suffered and were tormented by Roy's terrible uncertainty."

The day after I wrote my letter, the guards took Robert upstairs, and I could hear them making a phone call. I couldn't make out the conversation, but I heard Robert's voice, which sounded like something significant was about to happen. After all, I could count on one hand how many times Robert had spoken since we'd been taken hostage.

It occurred to me that this might be Robert's proof-of-life call, in which the kidnappers allow their hostage to speak on the phone to prove their victim is alive before a ransom is paid. The kidnappers always did one of these phone calls before a hostage was released, and I learned this meant someone must have agreed to pay the ransom. My birthday was just a few days away on June 23, and I prayed to God to give me my freedom as a present.

After Robert was brought back into our cell, I asked him if the guards were telling him he would be released. He finally said yes; the kidnappers had told him they were waiting for the money to come from the Philippines, and he would be released in ten days.

I hoped they were negotiating for me too. I always thought that he and I would be released at the same time—but I never got to make the proof-of-life phone call.

They took Robert out of the room again after lunch the next day, and again, I hoped they would take me as well, but they just slammed the door shut and locked it. I got the feeling that Robert was going to get out of here without me. When I pressed Robert afterward for more information, in regular fashion, he would not speak.

The day before my birthday, the guards came into the hole again and escorted Robert upstairs just after lunch. It would be the last time I ever saw him. I later learned that it was Omar who drove Robert to Baghdad, where he was traded for the ransom money.

The Philippine government reportedly paid one million dollars for his release. Afterward, Philippine officials asked the Saudi Arabian Trading Company we'd worked for to pay for half of Robert's ransom. The company declined, saying they would only pay half if I was released as well.

The two Iraqis kidnapped by the gang were kept for only a few days and released; the three Romanians and Munaf were held for 55 days and then set free. Florence and her translator were hostages for 157 days. Now Robert, my captive companion since day one, was finally safe at home after 233 days of absolute silence.

Now it was just Amar and me, in what would soon become a concrete tomb.

Amanda bought a cake on June 23 to mark my birthday, and she prayed for my release. Her birthday was just a few days later on June 26. I hoped she was doing something nice for herself, something that would distract her from my terrible predicament. But in my heart, I knew I had ruined her day.

25

REWARD FOR INFORMATION

B ack in the States, I had my own special-interest group working to secure my release—my family. Susan and Carrie were working hard to keep my name in the headlines and on the television news programs; they'd also created the Free Roy Foundation.

Susan prepared to sell her mother's house for forty thousand dollars to raise reward money. Amanda created a flyer that showed three different photos of me and offered the reward money for any information that would lead to my safe release. Amanda cleverly asked a Muslim scholar in Memphis, Nabil Bayakly, to help her translate the flyer from English into Arabic, and in both languages it read:

Roy A. Hallums—an American contractor, along with Robert Tarongoy——a Filipino contractor, were taken hostage on November 1, 2004, in Baghdad's Mansour District by a heavily armed resistance group. Roy Hallums' family is offering a reward of forty thousand United States dollars to any person who gives information toward his safe release. If you have any information, please contact Roy Hallums' family through their Web site.

Amanda used her contacts to get the flyers into the hands of service personnel deploying from the United States to the war zone in order to get them on the ground in Iraq—where those who might know where I was being held would see them.

After Amanda learned that former hostage Thomas Hamill was repeatedly asked by his captors if he had children, she allowed *The Commercial Appeal* (Memphis) to photograph Sabrina in the hopes that it might humanize me in my captors' eyes.

"We would turn on the news and people were getting kidnapped and beheaded over there; every day we were afraid it might be Roy," my sister, Barbara, said. "But in my heart I knew he was alive. If he was dead, the kidnappers would have told us by now, so Amanda and I clung to that reasoning."

Bloggers picked up the story, and my family utilized the blogosphere to get information on ongoing hostage-taking activities in Iraq, including my own situation. A popular Web site called the Jawa Report was the first media outlet to release my name publicly in the United States, having learned my identity after the Filipino government reported that an American by the name of Roy Hallums had been kidnapped with Robert Tarongoy. The site was created by a blogger who goes by the alias Dr. Rusty Shackleford (when he started the blog, he was an untenured political science college professor who wanted to keep his job). "Dr. Shackleford" launched the Web site in response to Nick Berg's brutal death in 2004.

"When I saw the Nick Berg beheading, it pushed me over the line and drove me to start blogging about the plight of hostages held captive in Iraq," he later said. "I was appalled by the gruesome video and that Zarqawi's group was actually promoting it. They were actually proud of their barbaric act." He continued, "They dressed Berg up in an orange jump suit—they were equivocating what they did to Berg with Abu Ghraib, where the prisoners also wore orange jumpsuits. I was also sickened that some on the American left were also making the same horrendous equivocation. When Roy was taken hostage, I was dumb-founded that there was barely any coverage of his plight in the mainstream media."

The Web site was getting three thousand hits a day in its infancy, and today receives about thirty thousand hits a day. "Dr. Shackleford" continues to use the alias because of numerous death threats from angry Islamists.

Susan and Carrie consented to several interviews with the blogger, who asked them whether seeing their dad's name on his Web site caused distress, or was a welcome relief.

"I remember the instant I saw my Dad's name in print and on the Internet," Carrie said. "My mind began swimming, and I had mixed emotions when I saw that his name had been released. I would have to say yes, coming across my dad's name on the Internet caused me distress initially, because prior to that point I believe there was some denial about it being my father taken hostage. Also, I had been told that if his name was released, potentially this would be a very bad thing for my father." She continued, "So knowing this, it was scary to see his name in print, and also going back to the denial factor, seeing his name in print made my dad's situation all the more real for me and therefore all the more difficult for my family. In addition to this, I didn't know what the consequences of both his name being publicized and the news coverage were going to be and what that would mean for my father.

"On the other hand, when I saw his name on the Internet, there was this sense of relief that washed over me. I had been told to be silent about the issue for so long and had not been able to express myself. I felt as though I was suffering in silence. So, it felt good now that others knew what I was going through—and I would be supported emotionally, I hoped, because I needed it.

"Most of us take time with our loved ones for granted," she went on. "You never know when a conversation you just had with your loved one could be your last. Time has become a precious commodity to me since my father's kidnapping. I have realized what little time we have with our loved ones on this earth, and how quickly and easily time with a loved one can be taken away. I don't take time for granted anymore, and for that matter, people either."

"You both have gone on record noting the frustration you've had at trying to get information out of the State Department concerning what they know about Roy's fate," the blogger told Carrie. "Has the State Department been more helpful since such major media outlets such as CNN have publicized your cause? What could they do to be more helpful?"

"No," Carrie responded, "I would have to say they have not provided more information or been more helpful, at least in my opinion. I've just received one phone call from the State Department this year and it was to tell me that they are giving the Baghdad police incentives, like flash-lights, to look for my dad. No comment."

"After some hostages were taken in Iraq, there were international outcries, mass protests, and national days of prayer," the blogger said. "Would you like to see something similar in the United States to protest what is happening to Roy?"

"It seems as though, when a report comes out about a hostage taken in Iraq, we all take notice, some more than others, especially if you are the family of the hostage, and then as quickly as the story was reported, it's gone," Carrie replied. "There is more coverage about the Michael Jackson trial than I'll ever want to see, and other trivial matters. I'm not saying his trial is trivial; molestation is a serious matter. But other frivo-lous things in the news are being covered, like Robert Blake singing at the top of his lungs because he didn't want to be interviewed. Things like that make the evening news, but nothing about my father . . . I find this to be an outrage."

While I spent my fifty-seventh birthday in the cellar pit with Amar, my family held a candlelight vigil to bring attention to my plight.

"Happy Birthday, Dad!" Carrie wrote in her diary, then added:

The candlelight vigil is planned for today. There is lots to be done. I took today off from work so I could devote my day to the vigil. Today is also Dad's 57th birthday. I wish I could be with him to celebrate it. But the vigil and the party afterward is the closest thing I can do since I can't be with him. I ordered a cake that says "Happy 57th Birthday, Dad" to eat at dinner after the vigil, and I plan on having us all sing "Happy Birthday" to him. I know that this will all be very painful for me, but healing and healthy at the same time. So I kind of dread it (the pain part) and look forward to it at the same time.

After the event, Carrie wrote:

I couldn't believe how many reporters were there! I had put up flyers everywhere and sent out tons of e-mails trying to get people to attend the vigil. The turnout on that end was okay. The most important thing was that the people my mom and I really wanted to be there were there. My good friends, my husband, a good friend of my dad's, my mom's friends, Gary and other important people in our lives. So it was a very special evening.

We had a table set up and everyone sat in an amphitheater-like setting near the beach facing us. We had a megaphone so our audience could hear us. We told stories about my dad. Some were amusing, some not; all were meaningful to us. We read messages from various pastors and reverends, and a pastor who was present, Rev. Nay, said a prayer.

We showed pictures of my father. I read an e-mail he wrote me, and I played a tape of his voice from a phone message. We lit fifty-seven candles in honor of his fifty-seven years of life and put his picture above the candles. I have a picture of this. It's quite beautiful. Afterward, we walked over to BJs and ate pizza. We saw ourselves on the news on their TV. The news stations really put together good pieces on the day's event. I really appreciated their coverage of our event for my Dad.

Susan found some comfort and inspiration in music, listening to a few songs over and over for guidance. "Music and praying to God gave me solace," she said. "I asked God to please get my prayers to Iraq." In particular, she fell in love with Ricky Skaggs's country version of "Somebody's Prayin'," a Christian ballad that describes angels watching over the singer as he travels through dark caverns and a barren wilderness, to protect him from dangers he cannot see. The song pretty accurately describes the predicament I found myself in, and the whole time I did feel that a lot of people were praying for me.

Carrie found comfort a different way, by writing poetry, including this poem for me, titled "Last Call":

> Talking about nothing
> Just wanting to connect
> Enjoying every minute
> Not knowing what might be lost.
> What I might have said
> Had I known
> How things might be different now
> And the future was known.
> I no longer hear
> His voice on the phone
> I see his face with a gun
> To his head.
> This is the image
> I see
> Each night
> As I go to bed.
> I see him in my dreams

Each night.
He's young and agile
For the most part
He's all right.

After Robert was released, Carrie began noting the details released by the media in her diary, although some of the specifics were not always accurate. On June 24 she wrote:

Robert is beginning to release details of his captivity, and he says my father was treated the same way he was. I've read all of these details off the Internet. No one, including the FBI, has ever called me and told me Robert was released or given me any information. I have to get all my information from the Internet.

Robert says that he and my dad were (and I'm assuming my dad still is) hog-tied and held in a pitch black, damp room. They have to relieve themselves into a container one time a day and cannot use a real bathroom. They are only fed one time per day.

They were beaten badly, frequently. They were hit in the head with the butt of a gun often. The guards would put a gun to their head and pull the trigger. Robert's arm was broken for a long period of time. His sight is now affected for being held in the dark for so long. My Dad and Robert were always blindfolded and cuffed.

The next day Carrie wrote that she wasn't sleeping well at night. "All I think about is how much pain my dad is in and how he is being tormented. I am feeling very depressed with everything I am hearing about my dad. I just wish I could do something to help him. It's getting pretty hard for me to do anything, but I have to."

Meanwhile, Carrie was cruising the Internet, looking for articles about Robert, when she came across a story that said that Rafael Sequis, the undersecretary for special concerns in the Philippines, claimed that his government did not pay Robert's ransom. Instead, he suggested that the Saudi Arabia Trading and Construction Company had paid for Robert's release.

"I didn't believe the article, but it still upset me, because if it is untrue, this statement could put the company at risk and maybe my father," Carrie wrote in her diary on June 26.

Carrie then called Bandar, and he said the company did *not* pay the ransom, but confirmed that Sequis had approached them to pay for Robert's ransom only. The proposal had been rejected. My company said that if they were going to pay a ransom, it would be for both hostages and not just for one. Frustrated at the rejection, Sequis had since declined to talk to the company.

"I felt like the Philippines paid the ransom, even though they were denying it," Carrie wrote. "Bandar agreed with me. It really didn't dawn on me what the ramifications of the Philippines paying the ransom could be for my dad. I don't think the Filipinos thought about it either."

The next day, Carrie called the State Department and asked them to make a plea for my release for humanitarian reasons, but they cautioned her that any public statements might have the opposite effect and end up raising the price of my ransom. The State Department official also told Carrie they'd met with Senator Dianne Feinstein's staffers on June 24 to discuss my situation, but they refused to give Carrie any details. Instead, they hid behind the designation of "classified information."

I've never seen that classified information, but during that period I can only imagine it concluded that no one knew where in the hell I was. However, with the debriefings rolling in from former hostages held captive with me, American officials should have been able to put some pieces of the puzzle together as to what group might be holding me. Also, I was pretty sure that Special Forces were looking for me, so my case file may well have contained information about unsuccessful rescue missions that would have been classified.

The woman at the State Department assigned to my case, Jenny Foo, told Carrie that Robert was being interviewed by the FBI. Carrie commented in her diary:

That was good. Jenny was someone that if you kept her on the phone long enough, she would give up some hints, which I could always figure out. She would never break confidentiality, I just did so much research on the Internet that I could usually piece things together with very little information. Plus, I knew I could eventually talk to Robert myself and ask him these types of questions if I want to get a straight answer.

I also spoke to Sue, my FBI agent. She is going to Baghdad to work on my dad's and the other hostages' cases. I'm really getting the impression that there is a lot of movement in my dad's case right now. Not too long ago the case was stagnant and the FBI had no leads. The Philippines were always in negotiations with a third party, a go-between of the kidnappers, but I have the distinct impression that they were not cooperating with other agencies until now. A government official who will remain nameless said they know they did something wrong by paying the ransom, so now they are cooperating more. I hope this is true because we have lost some opportunities to find my dad, in my opinion, when the Philippines paid the ransom. Most reports say it was eight million dollars, perhaps we could have tracked the money. If the Philippines had cooperated more with the FBI, which according to sources within our government say we can't force other governments to cooperate with us, then perhaps my dad would have been rescued when Robert was released and the kidnappers could have been caught. Perhaps the eight million dollars that the Philippine government spent to release Robert, and thank God he was released, could be returned to this country that has struggled with poverty for decades. I am definitely not saying I'm not happy Robert was released, but paying for one hostage and leaving the other behind, the other being my father, places my father in greater peril now that his captors have eight million dollars, in my opinion.

I want to go to Qatar to try and help my dad from there, but Sue keeps telling me no and that it is dangerous. I told her to take me with her to Baghdad. She told me to be patient and let the professionals find my dad. I told her I have been patient for eight months, I just want them to find my dad. Every second that goes by he is in pain and is being treated worse than an animal would be. It's hard for me to just sit around knowing that. She told me I can do good from here and that the media campaign by me and my mom to spread the word about my father's situation has not put my father in any greater danger and has not hindered the case in any way. She encouraged me to continue, and we will keep going because I believe her, that it is not hurting anything, and I do feel like it helps in some small way. I wish I could go to the Middle East, especially Iraq, and find my dad, since all of these "professional" knuckleheads can't seem to do it. I want results, no more talking, not that the FBI does a whole lot of that anyway. I've become like a corporate business owner when it comes to my dad. I don't want to hear "oh, we're working on it." I'm only interested in the bottom line. Is he free? Right now, no. So I am not happy.

I spoke to Robert Tarongoy tonight on the phone. He asked me to keep the conversation confidential. We talked for at least thirty minutes.

Susan called Robert's wife, Ivy, a few days after he returned home. She just wanted to find out if I was still alive; she didn't expect Ivy to put Robert on the phone, but she did.

"He was scared to death, the kidnappers had told him that if he said anything about them, they would cut off his fingers and kill his family, so he really didn't tell me much," Susan said. "He told me he was with Roy at times, like when they were making the videotape, but he didn't seem to think he was with Roy the whole time. He did tell me he thought Roy was still alive, and that's all I needed to hear."

26

BURIED ALIVE

After my birthday, the guards came for my lone companion, Amar. Omar was back at the house and was at his wit's end because Amar's wife still had not paid his half million dollars in ransom. The guard left the trapdoor open, and I could hear the thugs beating him and screaming on the phone to Amar's wife. Amar explained to Omar—again—that his wife did not have access to their bank account; neither could she sell their two houses or his truck without his actual presence and permission. After a while the guards pushed Amar back into the hole and slammed the door shut.

Amar told me afterward that Omar was nervous because American troops were operating in the area, and from now on they were only going to come into our cellar every three days to feed us.

The guards brought nine cans of sardines for each of us, a two-liter bottle of water, and some tomatoes and cucumbers and told us to make the rations last for three days. At least they cut the handcuffs that bound my wrists together for the first time so we could find the food in the dark and feed ourselves. However, they did not bother to cut the plastic bands off my wrists.

The guards also untied our feet so we could go to the bathroom when we needed. They told us we could now use the little portable camping toilet that was previously only to be used by the female hostages.

The toilet was the kind you would find at a Wal-Mart. It had a tan plastic bottom that acted as a holding tank, and a brown plastic seat with a brown lid. There was a small handle on the side that you would push to deposit the waste down into the holding tank. And for the first time, they gave us some toilet paper. It was the greatest luxury of my captivity.

When the guards left the hole and closed the door, we could hear a lot of scraping noises over the door.

"What are they doing?" I asked Amar.

"I think they are pouring concrete over the door," Amar said. "There is no way for us to get out of here now."

Sure enough, the guards had poured concrete over the only door leading to our hole in the ground. We were buried alive in that hellhole.

This photo shows the concrete that our guards poured over the door leading to our hole in the ground.

The six guards no longer stayed in the room above us day and night, blocking the only possible route for our escape. If American forces searched the house, Omar didn't want to raise any suspicions when the troops found six men loitering about with AK-47s.

I worried about what might happen if the family decided they didn't want to be a part of this anymore, and just packed their bags and left us in the hole to die of starvation, or perhaps suffocation. With the floor sealed up, it was even harder to breathe, and temperatures felt well over 120 degrees. Worse, though the vegetables the guards brought us were fairly fresh, I quickly learned that in the heat of our tomb, it would go rotten after the first day.

I could not see a thing, and I hated the thought of moving about the cellar blindly to search for my food—or the toilet. The last thing I wanted to do was accidentally stick my hand inside of it. As it turned out, the family would flick on the light several times a day for us to eat.

I had experienced so many terrors, so many beatings, and such abject humiliation that by now all I felt was numb. I counted the hours by the family's prayers, and I counted the days by the noise of Black Hawk helicopters that flew overhead at about nine or ten each morning.

Three days after we were sealed underground, I heard the sounds of an approaching vehicle; it sounded like the Suburban driven by Omar. A group of men were now milling about in the room above us, and after a time I heard hammers and a chisel banging around the hatch door.

It took them about twenty minutes to remove the door, and I could see faint hints of light from underneath the mask I was always ordered to put on before the guards came downstairs. I sat there obediently as the guards took out our waste buckets and the sardine cans, and brought in more tomatoes and cucumbers, nine new cans of sardines, and another bottle of water.

"Make this last three days," one of the guards said to me, and then they moved Amar out of the room and brought him upstairs to talk to Omar. I could hear them thrashing Amar, demanding that he call his wife again and tell her to sell the houses in Baghdad and Anbar, or Yasser would be killed and his body chopped up and dumped in front of the family's house. Amar pleaded with Omar to release him so that he could sell all of his belongings to secure the safe rescue of his son. Omar said he would think about it, and then he dropped Amar back down inside the hole.

The guards slammed the door shut, and I could hear the scraping sounds again; the guards were pouring concrete back over the floor. Then I heard something heavy being pushed across the floor. From the faint humming of the motor and the compressor, it sounded like the men had moved the freezer and were using it to conceal the concrete slab.

We were in utter blackness again, and it seemed that there was no hope we would be rescued. Even if American troops had a reason to search the house, would it ever occur to them to pull aside the freezer and chisel through the concrete underneath?

"Where are the Americans?" Amar asked me. "Why don't they rescue us?"

I was sure American forces were looking for me. Even though I was retired military, I was still one of theirs, and I was confident they would not leave me behind.

"How could they find us, buried under concrete, beneath this one little room, under this one little house in all of Iraq?" I replied.

"But they took over our entire country," Amar said.

I pondered this for a few minutes.

"Good point," I finally responded.

Amar told me about his kidnapping ordeal, how he and Yasser had tried to fight back, which just enraged the guards. He said it was probably the reason all of us hostages got such a savage beating when they were first brought to our cell.

Amar said they were first taken to a nearby house, and he was kept hog-tied on the floor of an empty bedroom, his head bleeding profusely from the pistol whipping he received by the kidnappers. "I was bleeding all over the place," he told me. "One of the guards called Omar and told him he was afraid I would bleed to death, but Omar told him to just leave me there; he said that scalp wounds bleed a lot."

Three flybys of Black Hawk helicopters and fifteen sets of prayers signaled that three days had passed, and I eagerly awaited the sounds of hammering and chiseling from above and the return of the guards to bring us more food and water. I carefully measured how much food and what food I should eat first (the vegetables) to last the full three days. I was now out of both food and water.

I waited and waited for the guards to come and feed us. After the sunrise prayer, I could hear the family going about their daily lives, but there were no motor sounds to indicate any of the guards were arriving, just the noise of the woman of the house, clanging her pans as she prepared breakfast for her family.

Lunch and dinnertime came and went. Still no guards, no food. The next morning, however, I heard the guards arriving, and the hammering and chiseling on the concrete began. It didn't take long for them to dig us out of there, but it felt like hours. I put my mask back over my head and sat down at the far end of the cellar before the guards finished and waited as they brought the food and water to us.

"Good morning," I said to the guard, and he answered me in Arabic.

"You did not bring us food yesterday as promised." I asked, "Did something bad happen?"

The guard didn't answer immediately, but after a few moments he said, "No, we just forgot what day to feed you."

As the guard took the portable toilet outside to clean out our excrement, I could hear him swearing in Arabic about the stench. I laughed to myself; I thought this a proper task for the thug. The toilet was very full, and I had been afraid that when the guards did not come on the third day to empty the toilet, it would overflow. Now that our bowels were no longer restricted to being released only twice a day, Amar and I used it frequently.

Soon the guard brought the toilet back into the room and left us a roll of toilet paper, but the roll was smaller, perhaps a punishment for filling the tank. I was starting to catch a cold and had been using the tissue to blow my nose, but now I needed to ration what little we had. I also decided to ration the food to make sure I had some left over in case the guards forgot to feed us again. (And they often did.)

The food we had to live on for the next three days included the nine cans of sardines, cucumbers, tomatoes, bananas, pita bread, Happy Cow cheese, and two liters of water in the Cheer Up plastic bottle. As an added treat, they brought us a piece of cake in a plastic package.

27

ROAD TRIP

Three days later, as promised, the guards came back. I sat quietly in the corner with my mask on as the men removed the empty sardine cans, banana peels, plastic wrappers and other trash, and the portable toilet.

But it wasn't just the guard's vehicle I'd heard approach the house this time—I also heard Omar's Suburban, and within minutes he was upstairs, talking to the other guards. Omar's presence had come to signal one of two major events—a beating or the release of a hostage.

I had a fifty-fifty shot at either.

The gang may have been skilled kidnappers, but I'd learned over the months of my captivity that they were inept when it came to negotiating ransoms. They could only handle one case at a time. Then, after one hostage was released, they would take a break for about a month before they moved on to the next case.

After Robert was released, I hoped that Omar would concentrate on my case next, but the guards came for Amar instead.

I heard lots of yelling and screaming in Arabic after Amar was taken out of the hole. I heard Omar hit Amar several times while Amar cried and begged for his son's release; he was practically hysterical. Omar called someone on his cell phone and put it on speaker—it was the guard who was holding Yasser in a separate location. I heard Amar speak to his son; as it turned out, it was Yasser's proof-of-life call.

Assured that his son was still alive, Amar was told that he would be released to sell all of his property, and that if he did not return with a half million dollars, his son would be tortured and killed.

I listened quietly with my blindfold on and did not move as the guards brought food for the next three days. They moved the portable toilet back downstairs, and then one of the guards spoke to me.

"Do you know the name of the man who is held with you?" the guard said.

"No," I responded, "I don't know anything about him, because we are not permitted to speak."

"Do you know if he is Iraqi or Iranian?" the guard asked.

"I don't know anything about the man," I responded.

The guard seemed satisfied and left the cellar.

A few minutes later I heard someone else come down into the hole, and he lay down on Amar's mat. The door was closed, but there were no sounds of us being sealed back in with concrete.

I wondered if something had gone wrong. I was certain I'd heard Omar tell Amar he was to be released right then to raise the ransom money. I started to ask Amar what was going on, but then I suspected this might be a ploy to see if I was lying about our talking or that I really knew who Amar was. So I waited for Amar's signal to begin a quiet conversation, a tap on my hand. The tap never came, so I never spoke. About an hour later, the door opened, and the man went back upstairs.

It had been a trap.

Amar was actually released, and I never saw him again.

Later that day, I heard the guards move someone down into the cellar. I recognized one of the voices as belonging to Yasser, and from the sound of it, another hostage was with him.

More food was brought down into our hole, and within minutes of the door closing, I could hear the sounds of cement sealing us inside.

Yasser did not speak English very well, but I finally tapped him on the foot.

"Yes?" he answered.

"Are you okay?" I asked.

"Yes," he responded.

Over the next few days I learned that our new hostage was named Ahmed, a young man in his early thirties. After he was brutally tortured and beaten by Omar and his thugs, they had determined through his screams that he was very wealthy.

When they unearthed us three days later to feed us, two guards came downstairs, and one of them beat Ahmed with a belt while asking questions about his business and properties he owned. Ahmed confessed that he was in the car import business and that he purchased expensive vehicles from Syria and Jordan and sold the cars in Iraq.

While Omar was working Ahmed over, to determine how much money and from whom he should make his demands, Amar came through with the ransom to save his son, and Yasser was taken out of the cellar.

Muslim was the only guard tending us now. He would sometimes sit with me while I ate with my mask pulled just over my nose. He would pat me on the leg and tell me that he knew I had been there for a long time, but that Omar would be coming soon to set me free. "We are trying to do the best we can about negotiations for you," he said, "and it is looking like you might be able to be released." It gave me hope that negotiations were ongoing, but by then I had heard this so many times that I didn't really believe him.

When Yasser had been brought back to our cellar prior to his release, Muslim had given him a small electronic game to play. After Yasser's release, Muslim presented the game to me as a gift; he was feeling very magnanimous about it and showed me how to play it. That is, he played the game while I sat there blindfolded, and he described to me how it worked. After Muslim left the cellar, replaced the door, and covered it with cement, I lifted my mask to check out the game while the light was still turned on. (Muslim would turn on the light before he came into the cellar and usually let the tiny bulb burn for about ten minutes after he left. When he wasn't there, someone in the family would flip the switch to light the darkened cell about three times a day to signal it was time to eat, then turn it back off after about twenty minutes.)

The electronic game was a cheap little toy that played several games a child in grade school might enjoy—racing a car through the streets while trying to avoid falling bricks; a basketball game; and some other simple games. But the toy turned out to be quite useless in passing time because it wasn't backlit, and as soon as Muslim turned off the dim light, the game went dark in my hand.

I set the game down and lay down on the new, thin mat Muslim had brought me to sleep on, and escaped my terrible ordeal through imaginary road trips in my head.

I started my imaginary trip from Memphis, driving my gray 2002 Ford F-150 truck; it was enough vehicle to take across the country to Los Angeles and could carry all of my luggage and the things I would buy along the way for my family and me.

I left early in the morning, but it was already hot and humid, even by Memphis standards, and headed over the M-shaped metal bridge that crossed the Mississippi River from Tennessee into Arkansas and headed up to Hot Springs in the Ouachita Mountains. It would take at least three hours to travel the two hundred miles from Memphis, west on I-40, and south on Interstate 30, and before heading back north on Route 7.

I've never been to the famous spa city, but I always wanted to visit, so while I was there in my mind, I may as well stop for lunch and take one of those hot springs baths they advertised on Memphis television stations back home. No, make that bath first, then lunch. I could imagine being in one of the bathhouses on Main Street that offered private tubs and steam rooms to soak up the thermal mineral water that Native Americans thought could cure pretty much whatever ailed you. And I had lots of ailments. As I drifted off in the tub, I could feel the pain easing in my shoulder and knee; the rashes from the sand fleas all over my body seemed to fade away.

••••

The flickering of the small light in the room woke me up; it signaled that it was time for me to eat breakfast. I ate some bread, cheese, and a banana, then used the banana peel stem as a toothbrush to try to clean my teeth. I poured some water out of the Cheer Up bottle into a small silver cup as both a rinse and a drink. I considered the small electronic game and whether to toy with it while the light was still on, but instead I settled back down on my mat and continued my mental road trips.

When I was a young boy growing up in Arkansas, my father would occasionally take on a second job on Saturdays, just long enough to save money to take the family on vacation—road trips that would take us as far south as Florida, or up north to Michigan to visit with relatives. It was a huge production that I looked forward to every year. Dad would get a new atlas, and Mom would call AAA to order more maps, as well as the Interior Department and local chambers of commerce, to request pamphlets. We spread the maps and tourist guides all over the dining room table and spent hours devouring the information and plotting different routes we could take.

Not long into my reverie, the little 5-watt bulb flickered off, leaving me in complete darkness, but by then I was already on my way—subconsciously—from Hot Springs to Dallas, about a 250-mile trek heading west along I-30.

But first I would make a stop at the Ouachita National Forest, nearly two million acres of beautiful wilderness, and take a hike. And that's exactly what I did. It felt good to stretch my legs as I walked for miles and miles through the mountains and down to a lake. I wished I had a fishing pole with me, and I added that item to my mental preparation list of things I should pack to take with me.

I normally travel very light; I never check bags on an airplane, because I figure the airline will probably just lose them. But even when I'm on the road in my pickup truck, I still travel light and will buy whatever I need along the way. I couldn't remember where I left my fishing pole at the house in Memphis, so I decided I would buy a new one on the road.

Back on the interstate, I would pass through Hope, Arkansas, and then on to Texarkana. I might stop there for a bite to eat, and I remembered that there is an antique auto museum I might check out.

It would take several more hours to reach Dallas, where I would stay for a couple of days and then drive down to San Antonio. All the time I would look for a good place to buy a cowboy hat or boots.

After San Antonio I would head out to West Texas and toward El Paso on Interstate 10. Since I was in the navy and had moved from coast to coast several times, I'd made this trip before—so I pretty much knew what to expect along the way. West Texas would be dry desert, and there would be nothing really interesting until I reached El Paso. There I would find the big western clothes store that is right on the expressway—that is where I'd buy the hat and boots.

As I continued my reflection, I remembered a time when Susan and I were looking for a motel room in El Paso, toward the end of December, but the Fiesta Bowl was scheduled to be played there in a few days. There were practically no rooms available. We finally ended up in a fleabag hotel for the night (it was still a lot nicer than my current accommodations, which were literally infested with sand fleas). I decided that, in my daydream, I would get a *better* hotel this time.

Leaving El Paso and going into New Mexico, I would pass through the White Sands National Monument, hundreds of miles of sifting gypsum on towering dunes. Heading toward Jornada del Muerto (a desert basin about a hundred miles long), the highway rolls through a lava field of black coils that Native Americans believed were made up of the blood and bones of monsters.

From there the climb begins into the Rocky Mountains in western New Mexico; I was headed for Tucson. My uncle on my dad's side lives there, as well as two of my cousins, one of whom is a captain on the Tucson police force, so I would stay there for a few days, visiting and catching up on family news.

The hours went by, and as they did, I continued my make-believe road trip. I drove on to San Diego, where I had lived for three years when I was in the United States Navy; I really liked that area.

Next I drove up the coast to Los Angeles and visited with Carrie and Susan, planning even more trips with them in tow. That was when Muslim interrupted my daydream with the sounds of chiseling around the concrete slab to bring us our three-day rations.

I was actually annoyed at the disruption. These daydreams were my way of escaping the nightmare—and the concrete tomb that kept me there. I was thinking about the road trips so intensely that it was like being in a trance—I could feel rain, wind, sand, and I could even smell the grass. Psychologists later told me that in extremely stressful situations, people actually do completely shut down their senses and go into a trancelike state to escape.

I definitely wanted to escape: the darkness, the heat, the stench, starvation. And the sand flea infestation. Even Muslim was so repelled by it all that he took us outside and hosed us down with the garden hose. It was a brief but pleasant relief. Then he brought in some more food, changed out the sleeping mats, and sealed us back in the hole with concrete. Once he was finished, the little light was switched off, and I was back in the dark—with my road trips.

28

CAMP SNOOPY

During the first week of August, Muslim told me the negotiations were looking good and that I would be released in ten days. But as usual, I didn't believe him.

Ten days passed, and I was still there. I didn't say anything to Muslim about it until a few days later. He said something had happened (but did not explain what) and that it looked like it would be another week before I was released. It gave me hope, although he was probably just telling me this to keep me under control. He likely thought that if he could convince me that I might be free in a few days, it would prevent me from doing something crazy, like trying to escape.

Another ten days passed, and Muslim said they were still in negotiations for my release. I finally stopped asking.

Toward the end of August, Muslim sat down beside me and started talking about his family. He had six children—four boys and two girls—but they were all grown and gone, and it was just him and his wife now.

Then he asked me if I had kids. I didn't want to answer. I didn't trust him. I knew that whatever I told him, he would report back to Omar. If I were caught in a lie, I knew I would be beaten and tortured. So I only told him what I had already divulged to Omar during my interrogations—I had two children, both adults, and I was divorced.

That piqued his interest, and he regaled me with the glories of divorce for women in the Muslim world as opposed to what Christian women experienced back in America. "Women are more protected in Islam," he said. "A woman can take away everything she brought to her new home, like a table or chairs, or the bedroom furniture."

I chuckled to myself. I knew that the man kept all of the property acquired *during* the marriage, including the children. For a man to be divorced in this world, all he has to do is say, "I divorce you," three times in front of two witnesses and the marriage is finished. But if a woman wants a divorce, she has to go to court and prove how bad her husband is, and even then, she probably can't get a divorce unless her husband grants his permission.

So, yes, divorce in Islam is better—for the men anyway.

Meanwhile, back in the States, the FBI was training my family members in how to react if the kidnappers were to call them directly to demand ransom for my release.

Although the Saudi Arabia Trading and Construction Company had offered to pay one million dollars' ransom for Robert and me, the kidnappers insisted that I was a spy and still demanded twelve million dollars for my release. Negotiations broke down in August, so the kidnappers asked my former employer for phone numbers to contact my family to demand the ransom directly from them.

My sister called the operation Camp Snoopy, after the recreation park that takes up seven acres in the center of the Mall of America in Bloomington, Minnesota. The park is based on the *Peanuts* comic strip created by Charles M. Schultz, and as a youngster I was a big fan of Snoopy as Joe Cool.

So Camp Snoopy set up shop in Barbara's house, and here the agents drilled her over and over on how to react to the kidnappers' demands.

"The trick was to act natural when they called, because under those stressful conditions, remaining calm would not be instinctive," Barbara said. "We practiced how I would react to threats from the kidnappers; I was to stress important points like his being a father and grandfather and how much he was loved by his family. I was to tell them that he was my brother, and I cared for him dearly, so if anything bad happens to him, all negotiations would stop."

My sister got along well with the FBI agents in Memphis assigned to communicate with her and Amanda on the progression, or lack thereof, in my case, and she had a system to get more information when she wanted it.

Barbara worked as an emergency-room nurse for twenty years at Baptist Memorial Hospital, where Elvis Presley was first admitted after breaking a finger playing touch football. The old Baptist Memorial is also where Lisa Marie Presley was born, and tragically, where doctors tried to revive Elvis on August 16, 1977, after he was found unconscious at Graceland.

"That was back when I was just starting out as a nurse when he first came into the emergency room," Barbara said. "It was a madhouse every time he came in there. We had to sneak him in the back door, and we put Reynolds Wrap over the windows so people could not see in his room. You could always tell when Elvis was in the hospital by the Reynolds Wrap all over the windows at Baptist Memorial," Barbara said.

The FBI agents, it turned out, were huge Elvis fans and implored her to share some stories with them. "They wanted to know all about Elvis. They wanted every detail," Barbara said, "but I told them this would not be a one-way street. I wanted to hear their information about Roy. I told them no more stories until [they promised to] tell me. The agents were just as nice as they would be; they were wonderful people of high character," she continued. "They had to close Camp Snoopy after Hurricane Katrina struck New Orleans, but they had prepared me well."

To reinforce her training, my sister wrote out in large letters the talking points she would use if the kidnappers called, and then she taped the lists near every phone in the house.

Slow down, mama, she wrote on one page taped to the wall. "I speak so fast, the agents told me I needed to slow it down and think to make sure I didn't say anything wrong. It was critical that no one talk about Roy's service in the navy," Barbara said.

Carrie knew that as well, and nearly panicked when one of my old Navy buddies posted a comment on her Web site mentioning just that. She took the comment down immediately and e-mailed him, explaining why.

"In a way, I wanted the kidnappers to call so that I could find out if Roy was safe, but in another way, I was terrified I might say the wrong thing," Barbara said.

Throughout my ordeal, Susan and Carrie did all of the public speaking and television interviews. "The FBI told us not to talk about it; they said it would make matters worse," Barbara said. "My fear was that they could kill him. But later, the FBI changed their minds and said it was okay to talk about it."

She continued, "Susan did really well on television, even though early on I was adamant about not going on television because at the time the government was telling us not to. But then they suddenly changed their minds and said it would actually help Roy's situation.

"I don't think Susan or Carrie will ever really know how much I appreciate all of the media interviews they did," Barbara said. "Their efforts kept Roy's ordeal in front of the faces of everyone in the government; they made sure no one forgot about Roy or how much he was loved."

Susan did more than a dozen interviews, and each day she called about that same number of people, anyone she thought could bring me home, including the Reverend Jesse Jackson, who prayed with her on the phone, and Rick Warren, pastor of the Saddleback Church in Lake Forest, California, who wrote the prayer for my candlelight vigil. She was on a mission for certain. "I felt like I had to accomplish something every day," she said, adding, "I never totally counted on anyone to help me, but I just had to keep moving on."

Her letter to Mu'ammar al-Qadafi worked, and the Libyan leader made a public plea for the kidnappers to release me. But when she wrote to President Bush, she got no response from the White House. When Bush came to Memphis for a meeting on Social Security, Susan used one of her contacts to request that the president meet with Amanda while he was there.

"An assistant from the White House called me," Susan said. "I asked if the president could bring comfort to my daughter. He said he would check and get back to me. He called me about twenty minutes later and said he spoke with the president and he said he does not meet with hostage families. He said it would be dangerous if the kidnappers found out he met with the family. I started to cry and asked why they couldn't meet behind closed doors. No one had to know about it; it wasn't something we would publicize," Susan said.

Dan O'Shea later said that such a meeting between Bush and my family would indeed have been very dangerous for me. If the kidnappers thought I was important enough to merit the president's attention, they would have raised my ransom to an even higher, impossible price.

After Robert was released, he urged Susan to call the Saudi royal family, and the FBI suggested she write the archbishop of Canterbury, the head of the Church of England.

Susan even mustered up the courage to call the kidnappers one night. Bandar gave her the cell phone number and told her negotiations had broken down between the company and kidnappers, and he urged her to call them to restart talks. She phoned them over and over all night long, and several times again, days later, but no one answered, and there was no voice mail for her to leave a message.

"It was ironic; they were beating Roy to get my phone number, and I was calling them over and over, hoping the cell phone at least had a caller identification function to capture my number," Susan said. "I hoped they would call me back, but they never did."

29

THE PERFECT STORM

S ome people thought I was dead. Since the video had been released in January, the kidnappers had done little to secure my release. There were no more phone calls to my employer, demanding ransom; it was as if I no longer existed. O'Shea presumed the kidnappers had carried through with their threat to sell me to Zarqawi, and he expected my headless body to turn up somewhere in Iraq any day.

But in June, following the release of a number of Western hostages, a perfect storm of intelligence had begun to form that would lead to my rescue, beginning with the debriefing of the Filipino hostage, Robert Tarongoy, on the day of his release.

"The first question Tarongoy was asked concerned Roy Hallums," O'Shea said. "The FBI and Hostage Working Group intelligence analysts asked, 'What happened to Roy, when were you both separated, or sold to different groups?' Tarongoy responded that he was with Roy 'just last night, I heard him coughing.'" O'Shea continued, "We were like, oh my God, Roy is still alive! Within three weeks, all of these different hostages were released, and in the debriefings, we realized that not only was he still alive, but these hostages were all held by the same gang."

Officials learned that Florence was held captive with me; however, the French government refused to share Florence's debriefing with American officials because of a rift between the French Security Service and an American official stationed in Baghdad at the time it was conducted in June.

Meanwhile, though, Robert's debriefing was further proof that I was still alive, and it gave new hope to the Hostage Working Group and Army Special Forces that I might be found.

One of the final key players who set my release in motion was FBI special agent Thomas F. O'Connor, a Washington field agent with the Joint Terrorism Task Force, who was sent to Baghdad later that summer to act as a liaison between the FBI and the military Special Forces looking for me. Before leaving D.C. for his new assignment, O'Connor sought out Tommy Hamill during an event on the National Mall in Washington. "I doubted he would remember me from Adam," O'Connor later said. "But it was important for me to meet him face-to-face before I was deployed to Iraq."

Hamill, the Halliburton truck driver who was kidnapped in Iraq, is the only American hostage ever to have actually escaped from his kidnappers; he was rescued after he flagged down an American army convoy. "It was an inspiration for me to meet him," O'Connor said. "He was proof positive that just because a guy is hostage, it does not mean there is no chance of being rescued." Noting my case in particular, O'Connor added, "Even if someone has been held hostage for nearly a year."

Dan Egli, a coast guard captain who chaired the White House Hostage Working Group from the Old Executive Office Building, noted that my case was, in his words, "our highest priority and first order of business" during regular meetings.

That my headless body had not been discovered by American forces led officials to believe that I was not traded to Zarqawi or hard-core

Salafist Sunni factions, but instead was probably being held by more secular Sunnis, likely former military officers serving under Saddam Hussein or Shia elements.

"Roy's case was particularly well-tracked because we knew exactly where he was abducted, the company he was working for, and by then, we had observed a pattern of hostage taking and kidnappings and extortions in theater," Egli said. "Al-Qaeda in Iraq leader Zarqawi was kidnapping and beheading hostages on video to traumatize and counter reconstruction and stabilization efforts. Sunni tribal elements and other criminal insurgent–linked groups were taking hostages for economic reasons, including extortion and ransom. We were confident—based on intelligence information—that Roy had been abducted possibly by Sunni or other elements and that they were seeking a ransom for money-making purposes. The bad news was that we didn't know where Roy was; the good news was that every day we didn't see him on a video, we were increasingly confident that they were holding him with hopes of making money. That gave us something we needed—time."

In mid-August, a young military officer working with the FBI on intelligence matters brought to O'Connor the name of a "person of interest" whom he suggested be located and interviewed. "The office had some information that was received several months before, but it didn't come to anything," O'Connor said. "We said it couldn't hurt to review it."

It only took a few days before the young officer turned up a vital clue that he delivered to O'Connor: somewhere in the western Anbar province, Iraqis were discussing an American hostage.

The operation was then turned over to the Army Special Forces.

The details of my rescue have never been made public, and it's taken me nearly four years to put all of the pieces together through discussions with military Special Forces officials who cannot be named, and other high-ranking government officials, whom I also cannot name because of the sensitivity of their jobs and the ongoing war in Iraq. But from what I can gather, with the military now in control of the operation, the

Special Forces were quickly able to pinpoint where the person of interest was known to be hiding. Under cover of night, they quietly and quickly surrounded the location and captured an Iraqi named Abd Al-Karim Khalil Hammadi, whom the operators nicknamed Stubby.

Stubby told the Special Forces that in his younger days he had been a soldier just like they were; he'd lost one of his legs during the war with Iran. Because he thought he was a soldier just like the Americans now occupying his living room, Stubby reasoned that the operators should just let him go. The Special Forces declined his request and instead demanded that the Iraqi tell them everything he knew about American hostages.

At first Stubby denied knowing anything about any American hostage, but the Special Forces had their own special way to make the man talk: he had been under surveillance before his home was raided, during which the Americans learned a little tidbit. Although Stubby was married, he had many girlfriends in his small village, with whom he was having affairs—a crime under shari'a law.

The Special Forces gave Stubby an option: either he gave up all of the information he had on American hostages, or they would tell everyone in his village he was an adulterer and expose his girlfriends and their families. Having a mistress in this conservative Muslim stronghold is a serious matter. Normally, the families involved will take matters into their own hands and kill both the woman and the man accused of adultery. So Stubby was quickly persuaded to cooperate with the Americans and was loaded onto a helicopter and sent to Baghdad for further questioning with the FBI. It was O'Connor's job to question the suspect.

"I spent several hours building a rapport with the man," O'Connor said. "I hate to say I hit it off with a hostage taker, but it turned out we were getting along well. He was not angry, and he understood what we were trying to do. Finally, he stopped the interpreter, Issa, and told him to relay to me that he was going to tell me something he had told no one. He had information about an American hostage. That piqued my interest. I showed him pictures of different hostages, including Roy, to see if he knew anything."

Hammadi pointed to my picture.

"He told us he was not there the day Roy was taken hostage, but that the kidnappers brought him and Tarongoy to his house in Baghdad directly afterward and kept the two men tied up on the third floor of his house," O'Connor said. That would be the house with the spiral staircase, with the western-style bathroom on the third floor—the Americans had captured the owner of the first safe house where we were held on November 1. It was a major break in my case, one that would quickly set into motion the final rescue attempt by the Special Forces.

O'Connor continued, "Hammadi said he was angry that they brought an American to his house, because kidnapping an American would bring a lot more scrutiny on the attack at the Saudi Arabian Trading Company. He said they kept Roy and Robert upstairs on the third floor and had them tied up there. However, his wife didn't want anything to do with having an American hostage in the house, so the next day he took the hostages out of his house and put them in a vehicle and planned to drive them to Fallujah to turn them over to someone else. But he encountered a roadblock operated by American soldiers, so he turned the vehicle around. He said they planned to take them to a mosque, but instead they took the hostages to his father-in-law's house, where they stayed the second night. The next day, the man told us they loaded up Roy and Robert and took them to Fallujah and left them with another hostage taker. He said he had nothing to do with the gang, nor had he seen Roy and Robert since then."

In fact, I was taken to a mosque the second night. Who knows— maybe Stubby didn't get along with his father-in-law, and rather than implicate the mosque, its imam, and his followers, he decided instead to blame him.

Although Hammadi said he had nothing to do with the gang and did not know anything about my whereabouts since I was dumped in

Fallujah, he admitted that he'd seen the Fallujah man he'd left us with just one week before he was brought in for questioning.

"That's when he told me that Roy was still alive," O'Connor said. "He said he saw the guy he gave Roy to and asked about Roy, and that he was told they still had Roy and that he was still alive."

However, Hammadi told O'Connor that even if American operators stumbled onto the house where I was being held, they would never find me. "In order to find Roy, he told us we would have to move a refrigerator and lift up the rug underneath, and then we would have to dig up a concrete slab that covered a hole in the floor," O'Connor said. "Roy was buried alive, underneath the house. I remember running from the interview room to tell my bosses about the new intelligence, that Roy was alive."

The mission was now back in the hands of the military, and the Army Special Forces began to look for their new suspect, the man in Fallujah who claimed I was still alive.

When they finally captured Majid Muhammed Hassan Al-Mashdanni a few days later, the conservative Sunni Muslim was drunk. It took several hours for the Special Forces to sober up Mashdanni before he could be questioned. Meanwhile, they moved his family into a back room and out of his view.

When Mashdanni was coherent enough to talk, he denied knowing anything about an American hostage. The troops took a photo of Mashdanni with a cell phone and then e-mailed it back to the Embassy. When O'Connor showed a printed version of the photo to Hammadi, the Iraqi confirmed that it was, in fact, the man he had handed me over to in Fallujah.

"We knew Mashdanni was the guy," O'Connor said. "People don't just make this stuff up and implicate themselves in a crime. He had admitted to holding Roy hostage at his house, so his credibility was very high."

But for several hours back in Fallujah, Mashdanni refused to answer questions posed by the Special Forces. So they tried a different tactic. The operators took his wife and children outside and put an American flag in front of the house and posed Mashdanni's family in front of the flag while their picture was taken with the cell phone camera. The Americans presented the picture to Mashdanni and told him that while he had been passed out drunk, his family was sent to Guantánamo Bay.

Mashdanni quickly admitted that he might know something about an American hostage and was taken back to Baghdad for further questioning by the Special Forces. Still, it took a while for the operators to convince Mashdanni that the jig was up. Seeing that Hammadi was clearly in custody (he was paraded past the open door where Mashdanni was being questioned) was an enormous incentive.

When Mashdanni finally admitted his part in my kidnapping, he described three safe houses where hostages were sometimes held, and the location of each. He described the exterior of the houses and the courtyard where guards might be posted. Mashdanni was then asked to describe the interior layout of each house—how many stories, where kitchens or refrigerators might be located, and what sort of bathroom facilities were inside or outside the houses. As he began to describe in detail one specific bathroom, the operators realized they had the exact location where Florence was last held. And then he gave them the most important clue of all:

"Look underneath the floor in the small building."

30

RESCUED

The Second Army Special Forces used the information provided by the two Iraqi men to match details given by former hostages. With all facts combined, it would not be long before Special Forces would be able to pinpoint the safe house where I was being held hostage.

Robert was the last hostage to tell the authorities I was still alive, but since he never removed his mask the entire time he was held in captivity, he was unable to accurately describe the farmhouse where we were held, except to say that he was in an underground cellar.

The missing piece of the puzzle was Florence's debriefing, which French officials still refused to share with their American counterparts. The Army Special Forces contacted the American military attaché in Paris and asked for his help to persuade the French Security Service to obtain a complete copy of Florence's debriefing.

The effort finally proved successful, and an Army Special Forces member was sent to Paris to obtain the document in person. In Baghdad the information was digested among the Special Forces operators.

Florence told her debriefers that when the kidnappers allowed her to go upstairs to have lunch with the lady of the house, she was also permitted to use the indoor bathroom before returning to our cellar. Once inside, Florence would remove her mask, so she was later able to describe that room in detail. In particular, she said that it was painted a very odd color. Most indoor bathrooms in Iraq are painted plain white, but in this bathroom the walls were a very drab green color.

It was the same dull, army green that I had seen adorning the bedroom walls in the first farmhouse where I was held near Fallujah. And it was the same color Mashdanni was now describing to the Special Forces operators as covering the bathroom walls of one of the safe houses he knew about. It was near the small town of Al-Mahmoudiyah.

It was 8 o'clock on the morning of September 7 when this last piece of the puzzle was set in place. Special Forces normally only operate at night, but they were afraid that the gang might move me to another location. The decision was made to move forward immediately with a daylight rescue, code-named "Objective Rock Creek."

With the location information provided by Mashdanni, a Predator spy plane was launched to provide live surveillance of the house; it transmitted the pictures back to a large screen in the Special Forces headquarters.

The operators were quickly briefed on the information provided by the Iraqis, as well as the live ground conditions; then the heavily armed men rushed outside to board four waiting helicopters—two Black Hawks and two smaller McDonnell-Douglas MH-6E Little Birds. Television cameras were attached to the helmet of a team member aboard one of the Black Hawk helicopters, and a second television camera was attached to the helmet of another team member aboard one of the Little Birds. The cameras transmitted live feeds back to Special Forces Headquarters in Baghdad. It was later rebroadcast at Central Command in Tampa, Florida; at the Special Operations Office in the Pentagon; and for White House officials.

The Predator spy drone would remain on station during the entire operation, circling high over the house that was now targeted for an attack by Special Forces, continually sending back aerial footage to Special Forces headquarters in Baghdad. As an added protective measure for the troops, an Air Force F-15 Eagle armed with five hundred-pound bombs was ordered into the area; it was also circling the house at a high altitude when the helicopters arrived. If the Special Forces met heavy resistance, the F-15 would bomb the area.

The helicopters flew over a patchwork of farms for about twenty minutes before reaching their destination.

The MH-6E copters were the first to touch ground on one side of the house, followed by the Black Hawks on the opposite side—but just before landing, one of the helicopter's tail rotors swiped a power line, sending a plume of smoke spiraling skyward.

Just a few minutes before all of the commotion, the little light in our cell was flipped on, signaling that it was time to eat. I was just about to pull back the ring on a can of sardines, when I heard the distinctive sounds of the Black Hawk helicopters. This was not unusual, because I marked my time in the hole by the flyovers of two Black Hawks around ten o'clock every morning. But this time I heard more than just a couple of choppers, and it sounded like the birds were directly over the house, and then like the house was suddenly surrounded. But just as quickly as the noise had descended upon us, I heard the sounds of the choppers taking off again, the whir from the blades quickly fading.

I wondered what in the hell was going on outside.

The helicopters had barely landed before the operators jumped to the ground and raced to the backside of the compound. Before the men could even scale the walls, the helicopters had lifted off and flown away to safety. This was very hostile territory, and it was too dangerous for the helicopters to remain here on the ground.

Although the Predator was relaying images of activities outside of the farmhouse, the Special Forces had no idea what lay ahead for them inside the house. Was it booby-trapped with explosives? Was it heavily guarded by Iraqi thugs armed with AK-47s? Regardless of the potential hidden dangers, these brave soldiers stormed the main house and the small building where I was trapped underground.

Side door of the house, one of several the U.S. forces stormed through to rescue me.

I dropped the sardine can at the sudden commotion above me, and my first instinct was to put on my mask. I looked over at Ahmed, and I could see the fear in his face. Whatever was happening upstairs, it sure didn't sound like the guards and their normal activities.

I wondered whether to shout for help. But what if this was an attack by a rival gang, there to steal the hostages and collect the ransom money themselves? It was a terrifying decision to make; this could have been another trick by the guards to see how I would react. It could also have been a rescue mission, and the sounds I heard could have been the guards trying to kill us before we could be rescued.

Ahmed and I were both so nervous, we didn't know what to do except put the masks back over our faces and listen, pray, and hope. I could hear lots of yelling, but I couldn't tell if it was in Arabic or English—maybe it was both. The sound of heavy footsteps thundered overhead from the family's sitting room and into the room directly above us.

Just as it occurred to me that the sound I heard was *not* the slapping of flip-flops against bare feet but the pounding of heavy boots, I heard the freezer being pushed across the room.

There was a truck battery on top of the freezer—not an uncommon sight for these Special Forces teams who saw these batteries in houses they had searched before looking for hostages. They knew it meant that captives had been electrocuted and tortured in the room.

After the freezer was pulled aside, the men ripped up the carpet that Mashdanni had told his interrogators concealed the small door that led to the underground prison. However, the concrete blended over the door so thoroughly that the soldiers thought they were in the wrong room. As one team rushed off to search the house again, the second team stayed behind to continue inspecting the room.

One of the men got down on his hands and knees to further inspect the floor space once covered by the freezer. He discovered a crack in the concrete, so he retrieved his Leatherman tool and started to chip at the concrete until he saw the outline of a metal frame.

"I think this is it!" he yelled to his team, who quickly gathered around him on the floor. A second operator pulled a sledgehammer from his backpack and started to beat around the edges of the concrete slab, dismissing any fears that it could have been booby-trapped. They heard part of the wooden door crash beneath them, slamming down onto the concrete floor below in the cellar, and the men knew they had the right spot.

I pushed up my mask and looked up at the opening in the ceiling. The air was filled with sand and dust. I could hear the men talking, but I still wasn't sure if they were speaking English. They pulled up the concrete slab and what was left of the wooden door, and pointed their assault rifles down into the hole, lighting the room with sweeping red laser beams. When I saw the guns' laser lights, I knew it wasn't a terrorist gang.

A man jumped down into the hole, and I watched as a flashlight beam bounced around the cellar before it finally lit up my face. I squinted my eyes, unable to make out any features of the person holding the light, but I could tell he was wearing a U.S. Army camouflage uniform and a bulletproof vest with a pistol tied to it. And he was holding a small machine gun in his hand.

"Are you Roy?" the man said with an American accent.

"Yes, I am," I whispered, my voice hoarse from nearly one year of almost complete inactivity.

"Jackpot! We've got him, and there is another man here also!" the soldier yelled to his team upstairs. He shined the light in Ahmed's face.

A second operator jumped down into the hole, with a spotlight on his helmet. I later learned it was also a camera, sending a live feed of my rescue from the underground prison to top American officials.

September 7, 2005, at the moment of rescue.
This image was captured by a spotlight/camera on my rescuer's helmet.

The first rescuer pulled off an American flag patch that was velcroed on the sleeve of his uniform and pressed it into the palm of my hand, which he clasped with a handshake.

"You've been rescued," he said to me.

I hugged him and thanked him. To this day, I carry that little flag in my pocket wherever I go.

Ahmed was so happy he was literally crying. He fell to his knees and exclaimed "*Allah Akbar*" over and over.

The rescue happened so quickly I didn't have much time to think. All I wanted to do was get out of that pit, and I was trying to make my way out of there when I realized the first soldier thought Ahmed was one of my guards. I turned around and told him that Ahmed was a hostage too.

The rescuers gave him a little American flag as well, then asked me if there was anything I wanted to take with me. I looked around the cellar. There certainly wasn't anything down there I needed, but I took the black and white *ghutrah*, the silver water cup, and the teacup.

Ahmed and I climbed out of the hole into the room above, and for the first time, we were not wearing the wool masks over our heads. The room was filthy; dust still filled the air from the demolishment of the inch-thick concrete slab that sealed us into the cellar. Trash and junk littered the floor that was still partially covered by a rust-red Arabic rug. The walls were covered with what looked like bedsheets decorated with large, yellow sunflowers.

A small wooden bench was situated by the doorway that led to a courtyard outside, and we were told to sit on the bench and wait until the area was secured and the helicopters could return for us. I quickly devoured the Gatorade and PowerBars the operators gave us, hoping it would give me the extra strength I would need to reach the helicopters.

A doctor came with the rescuers, and he asked me if I was wounded and whether I could make it on my own to the helicopters when the choppers landed in a nearby field. I was suffering from many wounds, but at that time my only concern was whether I could walk. Since we had been sealed for days at a time in the pit, where there was not enough room to actually stand up, the only opportunity to use my legs to walk upright had been the few times when the guard Muslim took us outside to spray us down with a garden hose.

"I think I'm okay," I responded, "but I will probably need some help if we have to walk very far. My legs are very weak."

I was wearing jogging pants but no shirt. One of the rescuers went back down into the hole and retrieved a white T-shirt the guards had given me and found some sandals I could wear.

"We've been looking for you for a long time," one of my rescuers said. Then he gave me a large American flag. Ahmed asked if he could have a large flag as well, but our rescuers told him that would not be a good idea. I added, "If you return home carrying an American flag, it might get you killed."

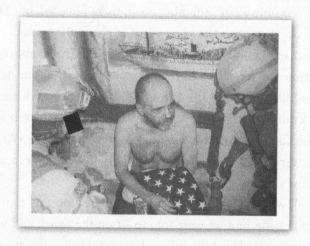

In the meantime, a second Special Forces team was searching for our kidnappers. At one time, there were as many as seven guards living in the room above us, specifically when there were nearly ten hostages being held in that small hole earlier in the spring. Once they sealed Ahmed and me in the room under concrete, the guards had been discharged; Muslim would return every three or four days to feed us.

On the day of my rescue, only the family members who lived in the house were there, and they were taken into custody by Special Forces: Hashim Muhammad Abdullah Al-Mashdanni, his wife, their five-year-old son, the four-year-old daughter, and a small infant.

Within twenty minutes of my liberation, I heard the Black Hawk helicopters returning, and two of the operators helped me to my feet and walked me outside. That was the first time I ever saw the house and the sandy courtyard. One of the soldiers gave me a pair of goggles to protect my eyes from the sand storm the helicopter blades would ignite, and then we walked about fifty yards to a plowed field and waited for the choppers to land.

For the first time, it dawned on me that I was actually being rescued. After 311 days, nearly a year after the gang attacked the compound where I worked, I was finally out of that pit. Soon I would be out of Iraq, and I would at last get to see my family again. For a moment I felt like I was moving through a dream, and for an instant I feared that I might wake up and be back down in that dark hellhole. That fear was dispelled, though, when the Black Hawks, followed by the smaller helicopters, came careening over my left shoulder; the troops on board were at the ready, with machine guns pointing out of the open doors in all directions. The Special Forces rushed Ahmed and me onto one of the Black Hawks, and within seconds we were off the ground, heading away from that miserable place.

Black Hawks—one of these helicopters carried me away to freedom.

"Open or closed?" one of the Special Forces men asked me over the roar of the chopper.

"What?" I asked.

"Do you want the doors open or closed?" he shouted.

"Leave the doors open," I said. "I've been locked away for a long time."

31

BARBECUE, WHISKEY, AND CIGARS

As we rapidly flew toward the Special Forces headquarters in Baghdad, I began to rethink my request to keep the doors open. A one-inch nylon strap across the open doors of the Black Hawk helicopter was all that secured the two Special Forces team members on board as it banked sharply over the Iraqi countryside below us.

My rescuers were seated in the open doorways, with their weapons pointed at the ground. It was only about a twenty-minute flight; all four helicopters arrived safe and sound. There had been no resistance to the rescue effort whatsoever.

I could see a lot of people standing outside of the buildings, and they starting applauding when the helicopters landed and our rescuers helped me disembark. They immediately took me to the dining hall, where a young airman offered me a bowl of Baskin-Robbins vanilla ice cream. I asked him for a sandwich, and he brought me a turkey sandwich, along with a Coke.

After I ate, someone found me a pair of tennis shoes to wear, so I was able to ditch the sandals, and I posed for pictures with all of my rescuers. Then they boarded us back onto a helicopter that would fly Ahmed and me to Ballad Air Force Base, just north of Baghdad, for medical examinations and our debriefings with FBI officials.

The first thing the medical staff did was remove the plastic restraints still attached to each wrist. They noted that my fingernails were white from dehydration and malnutrition—I lost about forty pounds while in captivity. They wanted to give me intravenous therapy called a "banana pack"—liquid potassium and vitamins—but I had already been through enough and didn't want them jamming a needle into my arm, so I asked them to bring me some bananas to eat instead. And they did.

In addition to the standard medical check, I asked them to test me for tuberculosis. One of the guards was always coughing when he served our food, and I was worried that he might have had that highly communicable disease. They laid me down on a gurney and brought in an X-ray machine. Fortunately, there was no sign then or in later tests back in the United States that I had contracted TB.

My knee was injured from my fall on the concrete patio in the middle of nowhere, but it was determined that I had no broken bones. However, I was suffering from severe muscle atrophy, a loss of muscle tissue that is caused from lack of use.

An Army major who was the psychiatrist with the Joint Recovery

Agency took custody of me next. He told me he was going to take me to some quarters where I could take a shower and relax for a while. Two guards with machine guns and FBI agent O'Connor followed us from the emergency room to a waiting vehicle outside. "Don't worry. They are here for your protection," the psychiatrist said.

We were driven to the VIP quarters, which was basically a small row of little trailers, and Ahmed and I were taken to separate quarters where we were allowed to take a shower and change out of our rank clothing. "Both men took about thirty minutes in the shower; they really needed it," O'Connor later said.

Afterward, an optometrist was brought in to fit me with some temporary eyeglasses. He popped the lenses out of a pair of aviator sunglasses and held several different glass lenses up to my eyes until we found one that allowed me to see farther than right in front of my face.

Directly, the shrink came back into the examining room to talk to me. His job was to determine whether I had gone nuts while held captive and whether they needed to immediately commit me to the mental facilities at the American hospital in Frankfurt, Germany.

"We're here to help you," the psychiatrist said. "Whatever you need, we're going to get it for you. People are going to ask you to do some stuff, and you don't have to do any of it. I'm going to be with you. If you want something or don't like what's going on, you tell me, and I will take care of it."

As I left the hospital, we walked past a concrete blast wall that protects the building against rockets and mortar fire. Everyone who had been treated and released from that hospital wrote their signature on the wall as they left, so I added my signature as well.

The psychiatrist took me to the small VIP trailer, where O'Connor and his boss, Anthony Russo, were waiting. We were not formally introduced at first. Neither man addressed me or looked at me; they acted as if I weren't even in the room. Instead, Russo asked the doctor if they could talk to me.

"You can talk to Roy, but you can't upset him," the doctor said. "If he wants to stop, you have to stop, and you can't ask him any more questions." The doctor then introduced me to Russo and O'Connor. Up to that moment, I thought O'Connor was one of my security guards.

A couple of chairs faced a couch set back against a window in the small, wood-paneled room. The carpet was cheap, and the room smelled like Styrofoam. A plastic, red and white No Smoking sign hung on the wall.

We would quickly ignore that order.

We settled into the cheap furniture; I sat in the chair next to the door, Russo sat in the chair to my left, and O'Connor made himself comfortable on the couch. The men then asked me what had happened, beginning with day one. As I told them my story, they threw in a few more questions here and there. About fifteen minutes into my debriefing, Russo asked me if I wanted anything.

"Yes," I responded, "I'd like a shot of Jack Daniels, a cigar, and a barbecue sandwich."

"Russo called Kevin Finnerty and Brian Jacobs and told them to retrieve his 'tactical humidor' from his hooch [trailer]," O'Connor said. "They showed up at our hooch with the humidor handcuffed to their wrists like they were carrying the 'football' containing our nuclear codes."

When they brought that thing in, I thought, *What in the world?* But when they placed it down in front of me and opened it up, there must have been sixty cigars inside, so we started cutting the cigars and getting out matches—everyone except for O'Connor, because he wasn't a smoker.

At first.

Russo told O'Connor he might as well join us because we were going to be filling the room with smoke—despite the No Smoking sign—and O'Connor would be smoking whether he wanted to or not. So O'Connor lit up too. Those were some really fine cigars. We smoked so much that the place reeked like an ashtray.

However, Russo told me, there was no alcohol on the military base, so a shot of Jack Daniels was out of the question.

"Give me a break," I said. "I was in the military for twenty years, and I know there is alcohol on this base."

Russo said he would have to ask the general about that, and I said, "Okay, go ask him." Russo laughed; he thought I was kidding. I wasn't. Eventually, I got my shot of Jack Daniels.

It was 1:00 p.m., and O'Connor told me they would not be able to round up a barbecue sandwich until after the mess hall opened at 4:30 p.m.

"Pork was hard to find in Iraq, but we got it just for Roy," O'Connor said.

I asked for a phone to call my family, and Russo said they were working on finding a satellite phone. I also needed the phone numbers, and asked them to pull my contact numbers for my passport. It turned out he wasn't exactly telling me the truth about delaying my phone calls to my family. Unbeknownst to me, the psychiatrist had told them not to let me on the phone to talk to my family until he gave the okay.

Hostage recovery and debriefings are very structured, O'Connor later said. "It can be overwhelming to make that phone call, and they wanted to control the situation; they didn't want him to suddenly be overwhelmed. When the psychiatrist prepared us to meet with Roy, he said this guy could be a holy wreck, but this guy really had it together. Obviously he had some issues, but he was not wailing and crying; he had it together; he was amazing. Physically, though, he was very weak," O'Connor went on. "At one point we went to get a cup of coffee at Green Beans, a coffee house that was as prevalent over there as Starbucks is in the United States. Because the ground was so muddy, there were board-walks leading all over the base, and at one point his legs just buckled and he almost fell off the boards."

The entire debriefing with the FBI took about forty-eight hours. I wasn't exactly on a sunup-to-sundown schedule, so the guys pretty much worked around my sleeping schedule. We would talk until I was tired; I would sleep for a while; and whenever I got back up and was ready to talk, they were right there with me, even if it was 3:00 a.m. I was used to lying still and sleeping more hours in a day than most people, and I wasn't used to being alert for long periods of time. I had barely spoken in the last 311 days, and my vocal cords were out of shape. Between the cigar smoking and my speaking for long periods of time, I quickly lost my voice.

The written briefing report filed by Russo and O'Connor numbered sixteen pages and ended with these "collectors' notes":

Hallums was made to wear a hood during the entire confine-ment period. Any physical descriptions were made from very limited visual exposure which was able to be made from either under the ski mask or during bathroom trips or video taping.

The dates provided by Hallums appear to match very closely with dates known by investigators. The dates should be given some flexibility and no information should be ruled out due to exact date inconsistencies.

Roy Hallums is an extremely good witness and may be able to provide additional information as time passes and the trauma of confinement lessens. Hallums's demeanor was very good. Hallums's physical condition was good but he is in need of nour-ishment and time with family and friends. Additional debriefings should be coordinated so they can be limited in number.

I was not able to identify any of my captors from photos Tom showed me, as I never saw any of their faces. Interestingly, the FBI asked me a lot of questions about my time while held with Munaf.

The Hostage Working Group was contacted minutes after my rescue, and Dan O'Shea—along with FBI agents—hustled to the site where I was held, to collect evidence. Asked later by the AP what kind of conditions I was held in, O'Shea said, "It was disgusting. I was thinking, my God, how can anyone survive in here without any hope?"

"He regrets that Roy was one of few success stories for the group," the AP said in a special report of my ordeal written by Deborah Hastings more than a year later. "The release of *Christian Science Monitor* reporter Jill Carroll, he says, was another.

"In some ways," the article continued, "O'Shea appears more haunted than Roy. 'I was there for two years and I still don't understand. Except that there's just evil in the world.'"[1]

I couldn't have said it better myself.

32

FAMILY REUNION

After the briefing was complete, O'Connor and Russo drove me out to the airstrip. There a U.S. Air Force C-17 cargo plane was waiting to take off at 10:30 a.m. for a flight to the Rhein-Main Air Base just west of Frankfurt, Germany. Originally, I was supposed to take a military flight to Fort Campbell in Kentucky, where FBI officials would drive me home to Memphis. Instead, a lieutenant colonel and a doctor with the Special Forces were assigned to fly with me from Iraq to Germany, then catch a commercial flight to Chicago and a connecting flight home to Memphis.

When we got to the runway, the cargo plane was parked at the end of the strip, but the pilot had not yet fired up the engines. We parked the car about twenty yards away, and as I approached the aircraft, I noticed that a video camera on top of a tripod was set up in front of a microphone at the bottom of the boarding ladder. An Army public information officer stood nearby and motioned me toward him. He was holding a piece of paper; it was the public statement the psychologist had helped me draft just after I was released, and the officer asked if I wanted to read it for the camera. Or, he offered, a general who would be coming by to shake my hand before I departed could read the statement for me.

Let the general do it, was my response. I didn't want to deal with it, even though it was a staged event; the media were not invited to my less-than-dramatic departure. I just wanted to go home.

The public information officer then told me that the general would stand by the stairs and shake my hand when I walked up to him, and then he would read my statement. He asked that when I climbed to the top of the stairs, I turn around and wave to the camera before boarding the plane.

I looked around the tarmac. "There's no one here," I said.

"This is for the camera," he urged.

A few minutes later two vehicles arrived, carrying some staffers from the Special Forces intelligence division who wanted to have their pictures taken with me. I obliged, and as we walked off to the terminal to pose for the photos, I jokingly told the Special Forces colonel who was going to travel with me that if I didn't quickly return, to send out the search party again.

After snapping a few photos, we did our little bit for the video camera, the general shook my hand and read my statement, and I did my part by turning and waving good-bye to the nearly deserted tarmac before I stepped through the doorway.

Shaking the General's hand before leaving Iraq.

The cargo plane was loaded with about fifty or sixty Special Forces soldiers, and two Little Bird helicopters were secured inside on the deck. As I entered, the pilot invited me inside the cockpit for the flight to Rhein-Main. I took a seat behind him next to a window and watched as we flew toward Turkey, crossing through controlled air spaces.

The sound of a woman's voice came over the transceiver, and the copilot, who was also a woman, said, "Oh no, Annie's working." She was referring to an air traffic controller for the government of Turkey, whom Air Force pilots around the globe have nicknamed Ankara Annie. Apparently Annie talked a lot over the radio. Constantly, nonstop; she never shut up. I quickly understood why the pilots found her so annoying. It was difficult to understand what she was saying, what language she was speaking, or to which pilot she was speaking.

Ignoring the constant babbling of Ankara Annie, the copilot turned her attention to me. She asked if there was anything I could tell her to do if she was ever caught up in a situation like mine—if a plane she was piloting should happen to go down over Iraq and she was captured and held hostage. Concerns about women being captured during battle had escalated during the war in Iraq, heightened by the capture of army private Jessica Lynch by Iraqi forces, and her subsequent rescue one month later by our Special Forces.

The copilot was genuinely interested in how I survived. I told her the only way to cope was to take it day by day, don't upset your captors, and just try to get along. If you're being held for ransom, that means you are worth more to them alive than dead.

Ironically, my ghastly ordeal would soon allow me to travel all over the United States, giving speeches at conferences and seminars and providing training for various levels of law enforcement, the military, and Special Forces. I've given lectures for the Navy SEALS in San Diego, California; for Army Special Forces in Fort Bragg, North Carolina; for crisis negotiators nationwide; and for FBI officials in Washington, D.C., Chicago, Newark, Minneapolis, Boston, Columbus, Nashville, and back home in Memphis. After that, I went on to lecture at the U.S. Air Force Survival School in Spokane, Washington, where pilots are taught how to evade capture or survive captivity. As an actual hostage, I had a lot to offer. In a way, my conversation with the copilot was my first lecture, as I shared with her my lessons learned, if you will. The first lesson was still *don't get captured*, but apparently, burying victims underground has become a new trend in the hostage-taking industry. As a survivor of the tactic, I'm a valuable commodity.

After we landed at the air base in Germany, I left the cockpit and went to the cargo hold below, where the troops were now moving about the plane and stretching their legs. The Special Forces colonel traveling with me told me these were the men who had rescued me, and they were to continue on in the cargo plane home to North Carolina. Before I exited the aircraft, I circled the helicopters on the deck, stepping over all manner of equipment and duffel bags, in order to shake hands with every single man and thank him for saving my life.

FBI agents were waiting for us inside the terminal, and they escorted us to a waiting car to drive us to the airport in Frankfurt. They said we would have to hurry if we were to make the American Airlines flight, and we flew like a bat out of hell down the autobahn, where the recommended speed limit is 81 miles per hour.

Once we reached Frankfurt, our drivers dropped us off at the terminal, and the colonel asked me to wait while he secured our plane tickets at the counter. I saw him pull out his government credit card to pay for the tickets, and then I noticed they were pointing and talking about me. Seems the government will only pay to fly coach, but the colonel had convinced the ticket clerk to upgrade me to business class for free.

As soon as I boarded the plane, I waved to the flight attendant.

"Is there something I can get you?" she asked.

"Yes," I replied. "A Jack Daniels and Coke, and keep 'em coming."

The Colonel and I parted ways with the Special Forces doctor after we landed in Chicago, and we quickly made our connecting flight to Memphis. I was exhausted, but I couldn't sleep; I had not seen my family in fifteen months, and I was eager to be reunited with them.

As we approached Memphis, one of the flight attendants told me that a horde of media were gathered inside the terminal, awaiting my arrival, and she asked whether I wanted to exit the plane down the Jetway to greet them, or avoid them altogether and make a quick left turn to exit through the outside ramp.

I chose the ramp. I still wasn't ready to deal with the press.

My family first gathered at my house in Memphis, where Amanda and Sabrina lived, and the FBI drove them to the airport to greet me. There they were frisked by security and taken to a conference room where they waited for the plane to land. Snacks, sandwiches, and soft drinks were spread out on the table as a reception area.

"I had seen pictures of Roy, so I knew what to expect," Barbara said. "Susan and Carrie were traveling on the airplane from California to Tennessee, so they had not seen the pictures on television. I told them that he looked thin, but that he looked okay. He was able to walk but was a little wobbly; he was talking and he was making sense."

"We didn't know what to expect," Carrie said. "We didn't know if he might be mentally challenged from torture; we didn't know how disabled he might be, or if he would be able to walk off the plane."

"Aunt Barbara told us we would have to take care of him," Amanda said. "I said I would take care of him."

The flight attendant opened the side door at the top of the Jetway, and I grasped the rail with both hands, because I still had trouble walking, and pulled myself down the ramp. Carrie was directly at the bottom; Amanda, Sabrina, Barbara, and Susan were close behind her.

We hugged; we cried; we laughed and hugged some more. With my family members' arms around me, they practically carried me inside the airport.

My arrival in Memphis.

"I was overjoyed," Carrie said. "He did look okay, and he moved really quickly for his condition, and he practically ran down the ramp. But he was super-duper skinny."

"We all went berserk, we were so very happy to see him get off that plane," Barbara said. "When the girls ran out to him, I said, 'Be careful; he looks a little wobbly.'"

"We were all so excited and overjoyed, it was a heavy load taken off all of our shoulders," Amanda said.

The FBI drove us back to my house and told me that if I received any threats, or if anyone odd started calling me or showing up at my door, I must call them and report it. There are a lot of weird people in the world who could react any number of ways to news reports of my homecoming, the agents said.

Several reporters did call for interviews and even knocked on the door right after I got home, but I needed a few weeks to settle in before I started doing interviews, so my daughters just took their names and phone numbers and told them I would get back to them when I was ready.

Back at the house, the girls were waiting on me hand and foot. I started to get up for a drink of water and they were would say, "Oh no, we will get it for you." When I wanted a sandwich or a Coke, they told me to sit still and they would get it for me. These niceties I would tolerate. But when I stood up to go to the bathroom, I assured them I could handle *that* on my own.

After Barbara left and the girls went to bed, Susan and I stayed up all night and talked.

"He showed me the clothes in the plastic sack that he was wearing when he was rescued. Oh, the stench!" Susan said. "It broke my heart to see these clothes, to imagine the conditions he must have suffered."

I still have the filthy clothes packed away in a trunk.

"We sat on the bed, and I cried," Susan said. "He told me that everything we did while he was held captive helped; it brought him home."

Amanda had refused almost all media requests, saying that she would only appear after I was rescued. So this time, Amanda and Sabrina went with us to do several television interviews in New York a few weeks later. We all appeared on *Good Morning America*, and Lesley Stahl interviewed me for a segment on *60 Minutes*.

"Two weeks ago, while all eyes were on Hurricane Katrina, something extraordinary happened," she began her report. "In a remote farmhouse fifty miles south of Baghdad, coalition forces rescued an American hostage, fifty-seven-year-old Roy Hallums. Hostage taking has become an ongoing, insidious part of the terrorism in Iraq. Two hundred foreigners, including over a dozen Americans, and thousands of Iraqis, have been abducted since the war started. Some hostages are killed, others ransomed. Roy Hallums was rescued. He was found virtually buried underground, blindfolded, with his arms and legs bound. He had survived ten months in utter darkness. Tonight, Roy Hallums tells his story for the first time."[1]

Well, it was more like the twenty-minute version of my story anyway.

Stahl asked me about the negotiations, and I confirmed that the kidnappers were asking twelve million dollars for my release. Asked about my family's counteroffer of forty thousand dollars for information leading to my rescue, I responded, "We were a little off, weren't we?"

"Roy's family was, at times, angry because they thought the military wasn't doing anything to find him," Stahl said before concluding the interview. "But now, they've been told this special rescue unit was searching for Roy the whole time. The unit is still looking for three more Americans. There's no telling how many kidnapping rings are operating in villages and cities around Iraq. Roy has now been home for two weeks, catching up with his two daughters, his granddaughter, Sabrina, and Susan. Psychiatrists have warned him he might experience flashbacks. He told us they have already begun."[2]

Finally, she asked me if I had received any "welcome home" phone calls from my congressman, senators, or President Bush. I had not heard from any politicians, and she asked me how I felt about that.

"If nobody calls, that's small potatoes compared to what I was in, you know. I'm just happy to be back," I said.

And I was.

It took a bit of adjusting, though, to the simplest of things—walking and eating, for example. The Special Forces doctor in Baghdad warned me to be careful about what I ate: "You have been on a very restricted diet for a long time. I want you to slowly get back on a normal diet, so at first, you should only eat light soup and Jell-O and not eat anything heavy."

I didn't bother to tell him I had already wolfed down a turkey sandwich along with the ice cream they offered me after I was first rescued. I ignored his advice when I ordered the Jack Daniels on the plane, and again in Memphis when I hit Corky's for some barbecue ribs only two days after I got home.

The girls took me to Costco the day after I got home, and I barely made it out of there without getting knocked over by frenzied shoppers. Ironically, we were there because Carrie and Amanda insisted on buying a shower mat because they were afraid I would slip and fall in the shower. Barbara made me hold on to the cart the whole time, and the next day she brought me our father's cane, which I used for the first three weeks whenever I left the house.

"He was really insulted by the walking cane," Barbara said. "But he wobbled every time he walked, and it just scared me to death. I thought that here he has come back to us without any horrible injuries, and now he will probably fall and break something. So I went behind his back and told the girls and my sons, Stephen and Michael, to stay close to Uncle Roy, to walk behind him in case he fell so they could catch him."

I really was pretty weak and unsteady on my feet, so Amanda and I would take walks in my neighborhood to help me regain my strength. It took days before I could walk any farther than twenty yards without becoming exhausted.

A month after my rescue, on October 13, I traveled to the White House to meet with President Bush. His entire Homeland Security advisory team was with him when I entered the Oval Office just after 1:00 p.m.

Entering the Oval Office and meeting President Bush.

I told the president that I believed I was kidnapped by a group who were former Saddam army or security, in the kidnap business to earn money for their tribe. He asked me if there were still Americans walking around in the Green Zone unafraid, and I said yes, Americans working for companies trying to get contracts in Iraq were moving around freely, going to meals or meetings about contracts.

The president asked many questions about my ordeal, and he seemed well informed about my situation, as well as those of other Americans still being held hostage, including Jeffery Ake, who, to this day, remains missing. He then asked me who had rescued me, and I said it was the U.S. Army Special Forces.

"Those guys are really great, aren't they?" the president said. "I have met with them before."

"They are great in my book," I responded.

I told him I was kidnapped the day before the presidential election but did not know who won until a few days after, when one of the gang members asked me if I knew the outcome. I told the thug I was not allowed to hear any news, and then he hit me upside the head with a pistol and said, "Bush elected again."

The president placed his hand on my arm and said, "Sorry about that. I guess they would have been happy if Kerry had won."

"Yes," I told the president, "they would have been, at that."

33

IRAQI JUSTICE

Special Forces soldiers detained the Iraqi family who lived in the farmhouse where I was rescued for three days before releasing the woman and her three children. However, the man of the house, Hashim Muhammad Abdullah Al-Mashdanni, was charged with my kidnapping. So was Stubby, who admitted to the FBI that I was first held hostage in his house in Baghdad, and Majid Mashdanni, who was captured by Special Forces near Fallujah and confessed regarding the safe house location where I was found.

Their trial in Baghdad was scheduled for March 6, 2006, and the FBI field office in Memphis called me and asked if I would be willing to testify at their trial.

"Absolutely," I responded.

"The trial will be held in Iraq in a few days. Are you willing to fly back to Baghdad and testify?" the FBI agent asked.

When they put it that way, I was not so eager to testify.

"No, I don't want to go," was my answer. However, I *would* go back there rather than see any of them walk away free without my testimony.

In the back of my mind, I knew that if my testimony were the only way these terrorists would be punished for what they did to me, I probably would have gone back to Baghdad or anywhere else. But the FBI offered me an even better option—I could testify via satellite from the field office in Memphis when the trial started. That was a deal, and I took it.

The FBI agent contacted me about three days later and told me the trial would start the next morning—at 2:30 a.m. my time, 7:30 a.m. Iraq time.

I showed up bright and early, ready to testify.

The U.S. attorney led me to a room and sat me down in front of a video camera. There were two television sets in the room; one showed me, and the other one was still blank. After a few minutes, the second television flickered, and I could see the Iraqi judge sitting at a desk in an office with a military prosecutor from the U.S. Army and an Iraqi prosecutor.

The camera in the Iraqi courtroom began to span the room, and there they were, the three kidnappers, dressed most appropriately (and to my absolute delight) in orange jumpsuits. I was asked if I could identify my kidnappers and, of course, I could not: I was blindfolded every time I came into contact with these men.

The lawyers and the judge questioned me for nearly an hour, asking the conditions of my confinement and how the kidnappers treated me. The Iraqi judge was very friendly and even invited me to his house for dinner the next time I was ever in Iraq. Such an open invitation by a judge in the United States would have surely resulted in a mistrial, but I soon learned that court justice is done a lot differently in Iraq. Apparently, it did not matter that I could not identify the men as my captors. They were convicted, and the hospitable judge ordered them to be hanged by their necks until dead.

There was just one catch, though: Russo called me after the trial and told me that Iraq law automatically granted the thugs a thirty-day appeal process.

It was exactly thirty-one days later when Russo called me and told me the three men were dead.

"What happened to their appeal?" I asked.

"Their thirty days were over," he replied.

Iraqi justice, at last.

••••

Munaf also got a strong taste of justice in Iraq.

Munaf remains accused of plotting his and the reporters' kidnapping with Omar Hayssam, whose bank accounts were frozen by the government because of financial irregularities. Their plan was to kidnap the reporters and demand several million dollars in ransom from the Romanian government. Hayssam would offer to pay the ransom himself to the kidnappers in Iraq, if only the Romanians would agree to unfreeze his bank account. That way, Hayssam could recover his funds and look like a hero as an added egotistical bonus.

Munaf is accused of convincing the reporters he could get them access to top officials in Iraq for interviews, and planning their whole trip. The fake kidnapping went according to plan.

Their initial captivity was clearly different from my own: I was blindfolded and tied up, kept inside a room with guards present at all times, beaten, and rarely fed. The Romanians and Munaf, on the other hand, were neither blindfolded nor tied up. They told me they were left alone in a locked room, fed regularly, and treated quite well.

But in a bizarre twist of fate, Hayssam was arrested just three days after the Romanians' bogus kidnapping, which prevented him from paying the ransom. Granted, the fake kidnappers were in on the deal, but they expected to be quickly compensated for their efforts, and when Hayssam failed to come through with the money, Munaf and the Romanians were sold to another kidnapping gang. My hostage takers. I later learned that that was why the FBI so carefully questioned me in the debriefing as to Munaf's behavior while he was held captive with me. They wanted to know how certain I was that he was a hostage rather than a kidnapper, whether he was treated better than the Romanians. Without a doubt, Munaf was definitely a hostage when he was with me; he cried the whole time.

And that's what I told the United States Supreme Court.

Munaf's lawyer showed up on my doorstep out of the blue one day in June 2007.

"Are you number 10?" the woman asked when I answered the door. It took me a few moments to realize that she was referring to the number my kidnappers assigned me for identification among the other captives.

I told her I was, and she asked if I would videotape a deposition on the Iraqi-American's behalf. They were preparing to ask the Supreme Court to determine whether the courts here had the power to prevent the American military in Iraq from turning over United States citizens to the Iraqi judicial system. The court had accepted the case, *Munaf v. Geren*, in December and combined it with another similar case, *Geren v. Omar*.

I agreed to testify, and we videotaped the deposition at a hotel suite in downtown Memphis. The lawyer wanted me to say that I knew Munaf was not involved in the kidnapping plot, but I really could not say that. I could say that I knew for sure that when he was with me, he was a hostage, but I had no firsthand knowledge of whatever happened before that.

She asked if I ever saw Munaf being treated better than anyone else, and I said no. She asked if he received better or more food than the other hostages, and I replied no.

The lawyer then asked where Munaf was held most of the time and where he slept. I answered that he was kept in the same room with me, except when he was videotaped and questioned by the kidnappers. He slept right next to me; his sleeping mat was so close to mine that it touched, and I described the close quarters in which we were kept.

I was asked if I ever spoke to Munaf and what we discussed, and I responded that I did talk to him, and that he often spoke about his family and how he worried about his wife having a miscarriage. Munaf had told me she had been through many troubled pregnancies before. I also told the lawyer that at one time Munaf suffered from some sort of eye ailment, possibly pinkeye. She asked if our captors ever gave him medicine to treat his condition, and I replied that they did not.

Did Munaf ever act like he was part of the gang? she then wanted to know. I said that he did not. She asked if I thought Munaf was a hostage. I said that when he was with me, he was a hostage just like the rest of us and had the same fear of being tortured and killed.

Finally, she asked if I thought Munaf was involved in the kidnapping of the Romanians. I said I did not know anything about what he did before he showed up in the hole with me, but the entire period he was with me, he was a hostage and was treated the same as me, which was not well at all.

The habeas corpus case was argued before the Supreme Court on March 25, and their decision was handed down on June 12. The court found that Munaf, an Iraqi with American citizenship, had "voluntarily traveled to Iraq and allegedly committed crimes there," and that he was captured by military forces operating as part of the Multi-National Force–Iraq (MNF–I) and given hearings before the MNF–I tribunals composed of American officers, who concluded that Munaf "posed threats to Iraqi's security."[1]

Chief Justice John G. Roberts Jr. wrote in the decision that "Iraq has a sovereign right to prosecute [Munaf] for crimes committed on its soil, even if its criminal process does not come with all the rights guaranteed by the Constitution."[2]

"The Court's decision ensures that the Iraqi courts can proceed with the prosecution of the habeas petitioners for serious offenses committed in Iraq," the Justice Department said in a statement.[3]

As of the writing of this book, Munaf remains behind bars in an Iraqi jail, charged with his own kidnapping and that of the Romanian reporters.

34

AMERICAN FLAG

Carrie and Amanda made a promise to themselves that after I was rescued they would make up for all of the birthdays that we missed together.

They got a little carried away.

Carrie was in Memphis to participate in a new reality-TV program hosted by country music star Kelly Lang, called *Give a Living Rose*, which was producing a segment on my ordeal.

At least that's what I told the girls.

The show paid for Carrie's plane ticket to Memphis, and her hotel room as well. Tom O'Connor and his wife, Jean, also flew in from Washington to participate in the show.

We all gathered at Corky's Barbecue on a hot August night in 2008 for dinner. A photographer from the show tagged along to videotape it for the program. Amanda was there with Sabrina and her young son, Hayden, who was born after my release. Carrie held little Reid, my grandson, who was just a few months old. O'Connor and Jean were there as well, along with my coauthor, Audrey Hudson. A girl I knew from high school, Janice Deas, was my date for the evening.

As an appetizer of various barbecue treats was served, O'Connor regaled us all with humorous stories about my debriefing, including the great cigar smoke-out.

"The first things Roy asked for were barbecue, Jack Daniels sour mash whiskey, and some cigars, and not necessarily in that order," O'Connor said. "He had hardly spoken in a year, but there he was, puffing away on the cigars. When I later learned Roy was from Memphis, his requests made complete sense to me, but in the Muslim world of Iraq, all alcohol, tobacco, and most certainly a pork sandwich were nearly impossible to acquire. Pork was hard to get in Iraq, but we got it just for him. But after eating Memphis barbecue, I am thoroughly ashamed of the sorry quality of barbecue we managed to scrounge up." Everyone laughed.

After we wolfed down the meal, the waitstaff brought out a cake and sang "Happy Birthday" to me. I just sat there, unfazed, and played along for my girls and my grandchildren. It wasn't the first time they'd pulled this stunt, nor would it be the last. Whenever the whole family eats out, the girls make sure I get a birthday cake at the end of every meal.

After individual interviews with Carrie, Amanda, and O'Connor, the program staged a cocktail party to videotape family and friends in attendance when the surprise announcement was made.

The party was originally planned to be held on the rooftop of the chic Madison Hotel overlooking the Mississippi River, but it was interrupted by the remnants of Tropical Storm Fay, so it was moved inside at the last moment. Barbara was there, along with dozens of old high school friends who boisterously told stories about me; some of them were even true. Multicolored roses adorned the party room to symbolize the theme of the program.

The director called everyone downstairs into the hotel lobby and arranged us all for the cameras in the stylized living room setting around a grand piano for the final scene they would shoot for the program.

I mentally rehearsed what I was going to say, but I was still nervous. With Amanda and Carrie on one side of me, and O'Connor (representing the hundreds of people in the government who worked on my rescue) standing to my left, I announced to our forty guests that the program was not going to be about me, but rather it was to honor and thank those who had had a profound effect on my life: Carrie, Amanda, and O'Connor. Tears formed in my daughters' eyes, and O'Connor's jaw nearly hit the floor.

The girls quickly regained their composure when I reached underneath a cushion on the sofa behind me and produced two jewelry boxes decorated in Tiffany Blue, a color instantly recognized by women across the globe. The boxes contained silver necklaces, each having a diamond centered inside a heart. As a federal employee, O'Connor is not allowed to accept gifts of any real value, but we did give him a little wooden box with an inscription thanking him for his role that led to my rescue.

It was a night that none of them will forget.

••••

The question I get most often is, how did you manage to survive? Some people think it was my ability to compartmentalize every day, to just survive hour by hour.

"Roy was in shut-down mode for months after he got home. He would shake, and he refused to watch the videotape his kidnappers forced him to help make," Susan said. "But he snapped back quickly. He was always a very patient person and laid-back. As for me, I can't stand to sit in a doctor's office for ten minutes, but Roy could sit there all day long and not get aggravated. He had a strong will to live, and he was determined to see his family again."

On *60 Minutes*, Lesley Stahl reported, "Roy told us his story with little emotion, no matter how horrendous the details, as if what happened to him had happened to someone else. He seems numb."[1]

The truth is, I was born in Arkansas, and my family did not have a lot of money then, and like most people at the time, we did not have an indoor bathroom. Our grandparents didn't have indoor plumbing, and some relatives didn't have electricity, so going without these luxuries for such a long period of time wasn't too much of a strain on me.

Our parents also raised us to have positive attitudes, strong moral values, and a can-do attitude. My father forbade a certain four-letter word from our vocabularies—*can't*.

"If we ever said that word, we got a good talking-to," Barbara said, then added, "Roy is very patient and sees things from other people's point of view; he's the most patient person I ever met in my life. I've never seen him get mad or lose his temper and scream at someone. He has a good sense of who he is and what he can accomplish in life. The road trips he planned in his head to escape his terrible ordeal probably saved his sanity."

Agent Tom O'Connor came to me sometime later and told me that he was going to be attending Air Force Survival School in Spokane, part of which included hostage rescue training. Part of that training, he was told beforehand, would involve his being blindfolded and handcuffed like a hostage for about four hours. He asked me for any advice I might have to get through the ordeal. "Imagine being in that situation for month after month and not knowing how long it will last," I told him.

"It just about drove me nuts," O'Connor said of being blindfolded. "All I could think was *how Roy could have survived this for months on end without going insane.* But Roy is just a laid-back and easygoing guy. I don't think you could rile him up about anything; he just seems to snap back out of any situation. He never got an opportunity to escape, but he was determined to survive, and he did."

••••

My old housemate, Zein, contacted me in September of 2008 and asked me to move back to the Middle East and take a job working for him in Beirut.

"No, thanks," I responded. Fifty American contractors have been kidnapped since the war in Iraq began. I remain the only one who has been rescued.

After the ransom was paid for my fellow hostages, the guards actually gave them going-away presents: new clothes, a pen, maybe, or a half-used bottle of perfume. I got nothing from my guards—but I did get an American flag from my rescuers.

That was the best gift of all.

ACKNOWLEDGMENTS

There were hundreds of dedicated government personnel who worked on my case tirelessly, day in and day out, including the FBI, U.S. Army Special Forces, the Hostage Working Group in Baghdad, the White House, and the U.S. State Department. These people continued their work even after it was assumed I was dead and there was no hope in ever recovering me alive. Their professionalism and interest in my case eventually led to my rescue and return to my family, and for that, I am eternally grateful.

I want to give special thanks to FBI special agents Tom O'Connor, Anthony Russo, and Keli Sligh, as well as Naval Criminal Investigative Service agent Rick Yell, for their faith in continuing my case and their assistance to my family.

I am also very grateful to the communities of Memphis, Tennessee, and Corona, California, for their support of my family throughout my ordeal.

I want to thank my family for their strength and courage, and for all of the work they did to help bring me back home.

We would also like to thank Thomas Nelson Publishers for their faith in this book, in particular, publisher Joel Miller and all of the editors (Kristen Parrish, Heather Skelton, and Jamie Chavez) who brought this project to fruition. And to my good friend, T. G. Sheppard, who encouraged me to tell my story. Thank you for all of your support.

—Roy Hallums

••••

I especially want to thank Roy for allowing me into his life and his head, and for sharing every last detail of his brutal kidnapping and historic rescue. It was the exclusive interview of a lifetime.

I want to thank John Sopko, Sharon Behn, Dan O'Shea, and Jeff Denning, who were all a tremendous help with their tireless research, fact-checking, and in some cases, sharing of confidential sources.

To my colleagues at the *Washington Times*: a special thank-you to assistant managing editor Carlton Bryant for his help and support, as well as managing editor David Jones and executive editor John Solomon for their encouragement.

Thanks to my family for their support, including my girls, Jenny Lyne and Tricia; my father, Jim Hudson, and his wife, Shelagh; my brothers, Jackson and Cliff Latta, and Cliff's wife, Paula; my nephew, Adam; and my niece, Holley, who put her psychology degree to good use.

Above all, I could not have reached the finishing line without the love and support of my mother, Ann Latta, and my husband, Paul Flanagan. Mom's meticulous editing notes were essential, and I am appreciative of her never-ending confidence in me. And to my wonderful husband, Paul, chief fact-checker, I will be forever grateful for your love, support, and patience.

—Audrey Hudson

NOTES

Chapter 5: The Mosque

1. Wahhabi is a very conservative form of Sunni Islam.

Chapter 8: The Kidnapping Business

1. Reuters, "American, Nepali kidnapped," 1 November 2004.
2. "Gunmen seize six hostages in Iraq," BBC News, 2 November 2004, http://
   news.bbc
   .co.uk/2/hi/middle_east/3972569.stm.
3. "American, Asian among six people kidnapped in Baghdad," Agence France-
   Presse, 1 November 2004, LexisNexis News, http://www.lexisnexis.com.
4. "Three hostages taken in raid by kidnappers," CBS Evening News, 1
   November 2004, CBS News Transcripts (accessed 16 September 2008).
5. Edward Wong and Richard A. Oppel Jr., "THE 2004 CAMPAIGN:
   INSURGENCY; American Is Among 4 Captives Seized in Baghdad
   Kidnapping," *New York Times*, 2 November 2004, http://query.nytimes.com/
   gst/fullpage.html?res=9E04E7DE1F3DF931A35752C1A9629C8B63.
6. Mariam Fam (Associated Press), "Six killed in car bomb near Iraqi Ministry
   of Education: kidnappers release two Iraqi guards abducted with American,"
   SignOnSanDiego.com (by the *Union-Tribune*), 2 November 2004, http://
   www.signonsandiego.com/news/world/iraq/20041102-0512-iraq.html.
7. Karl Penhaul, Kianne Sadeq, Kevin Flower, and Mohammed Tawfeeq,
   "American among 6 kidnapped in Baghdad," *CNN.com*, 1 November

2004, http://www.cnn.com/2004/WORLD/meast/11/01/iraq.main/index
.html.

8. "U.S. citizen, five others kidnapped in Iraq on eve of US elections," Agence
France Presse, 1 November 2004, LexisNexis (accessed 16 September 2008).

Chapter 14: Rules of the House

1. *CNN Live Saturday*, transcript of program aired 18 December 2004,
http://premium.cnn.com/TRANSCRIPTS/0412/18/cst.04.html.

2. Ibid.

3. Lisa O'Neill Hill, "Hostage's ex-wife keeps hope," *The Press Enterprise*
(Riverside, CA), 21 December 2004. Article available at http://www.pe.com/.

Chapter 23: Munaf

1. Associated Press, "Romanian journalist recounts 8-week kidnapping ordeal
in Iraq," 29 May 2005, LexisNexis.

Chapter 24: Another Ransom Paid

1. "France denies paying ransom to free journalist," *Guardian*, 13 June
2005, http://www.guardian.co.uk/media/2005/jun/13/pressandpublishing
.iraq.

2. "Brave Heart, A happy ending," *Time*, 10 October 2005, http://www.time.
com/time/europe/hero2005/aubenas.html.

3. "Profile: Florence Aubenas," BBC News Europe, 12 June 2005,
www.news.bbc.co.uk/2/hi/europe/4085194.stm (accessed 22 January 2009).

Chapter 31: Barbecue, Whiskey, and Cigars

1. Deborah Hastings (Associated Press), "Come, or We'll Kill You – Part II" AII
POW-MIA InterNetwork, 25 December 2006, http://www.aiipowmia.com/
inter26/in251206killyoupt2.html.

Chapter 32: Family Reunion

1. Lesley Stahl, "Hostage: Roy Hallums discusses spending 10 months in
captivity in Iraq and his dramatic rescue by US forces," *60 Minutes*, 25
September 2005, CBS News transcripts (accessed 16 September 2008).
See http://www.cbsnews.com/stories/2005/09/22/60minutes/main879605
.shtml.

2. Ibid.

Chapter 33: Iraqi Justice

1. *Munaf et al v. Geren, Secretary of the Army, et al.*, Supreme Court of the United States Certiorari to the United States Court of Appeals for the District Of Columbia Circuit, no. 06–1666, 12 June 2008, http://www.supremecourtus.gov/opinions/07pdf/06-1666.pdf, 1.
2. Ibid., 4.
3. Carrie Johnson, "Ability to Challenge Transfer to Foreign Custody Is Limited," *Washington Post*, 13 June 2008, A03, http://www.washingtonpost.com/wp-dyn/content/article/2008/06/12/AR2008061203653.html.

Chapter 34: American Flag

1. Stahl, "Hostage."

ABOUT THE AUTHOR

R oy Hallums, a retired U.S Navy Commander, worked as a civilian contractor in Iraq where his company provided food for the American army in Baghdad. He was taken captive in 2004 and was freed by coalition forces in 2005.